Lewy, Mom, and Me

Lewy, Mom, and Me

a caregiver's story

Peggy Bushy

ISBN: 1537771027
ISBN 13: 9781537771021
Library of Congress Control Number: 2016915726
CreateSpace Independent Publishing Platform
North Charleston, South Carolina

bushy books
Cover Design: Forlivesi Photography
2016

For my mothers:
Mary, Mary, Margaret, Margaret, Sally, and
Jean Francesca

Acknowledgments

I WOULD LIKE to thank all the wonderful teachers, passed and present, who blessed me with encouraging words.

Thank you to all the admirable people who cared for my mother. You will all have a special place in my heart. Once again, thank-you Anna.

Thank you to Beth Breen-Santheson for keeping me balanced.

A huge thank you to my test readers and editors: Kaela Amaral, Betty Breen, Tom Bushy, Jennifer MacDonald, T.M. Murphy, Leanne Rabesa and Lynn Sciarretta.

I also want to thank the many family and friend readers who cheered me on along the way: Lisa Amaral, Marie Bartram, Lisa Bushy, Anne Marie Carr, Cutsy Conroy, Susie DeGirolamo, Mary Kobey, Theresa Nyhan, Damien Palanza, Amy Renna, Kerry Smith, and Sarah Walsh. Thank you, thank you, thank you!

To my aunties, Cutsy, Mary Joan, Susie, and Aunt Sue, thank you for all the help with Mom.

Thanks to my Palanza Family for all the kind words and hugs. I love being a part of this great big beautiful bunch. Thank you Bushy Family for all your love and support.

Thank you to Sarah Valentini and P.J. Sowden for the respites.

Thanks to the lunch angels who filled in while I was away, my aunties, Donna Domingos, Rita Pacheco, and Bobby and Stephen Smith. Love you T.

An immeasurable thank-you goes out to my life lines, Lisa Amaral for the original cover design and support on demand, and Marie Bartram, who held my hand through this journey. I'd be lost without you two.

Thank you to my children, Tom, Traci, Michael, Becca, Joseph, and Leslie, for all the love and support you gave to Nonni, Dad, and me. I am exceedingly proud to know you all.

To my perfect grandchildren, your hugs are the best medicine for whatever ails me.

- T3, you are the kindest child I've ever met.
- Nathan, thank you for reminding me that the world is a beautiful place.
- Lukas, thank you for keeping me honest and filling my life with laughter.
- Peyton Margaret, thank you for being a girl!
- Thank you to my sweet Dolly Angel for letting me use your name.

An astronomical thank you to God and the angels and saints for giving me so many wonderful blessings, especially the gifts of faith, family, and friends and for blessing me with a beautiful, legendary mother. Thank you, God, as well for my karmic mate, Tom, who caught me, carried me, and walked with me through this journey. I am forever grateful—and I'm all yours.

ONE

———— ∿ ————

Enjoy the good times; they won't always be there.

—Francesca Jean

Francesca sat around the massive wooden kitchen table with sixteen other strong-minded children. Fifteen of them lived there, and the other two were friends of her brothers who wished they lived there. Each had a spoon, most had chairs, and none of them had plates. Tonight, plates weren't necessary. It was Saturday night—polenta night—a prelude to the Italian family's Sunday dinner feast. Polenta, the one-pot wonder that easily filled her children's bellies, provided Mama with time to work on the multilayered meal she was preparing for the next day. The long hand-made table hosted a huge wooden board with heaps of the bright yellow cornmeal piled high. The bulls-eye in the middle of the polenta housed a number of prized meatballs topped with extra sauce and luscious, hand-grated parmesan cheese, and the first one to eat their way through the polenta to the middle of the board got the reward. The older boys always won. Love, laughter, and chatter filled the room until the crowd thinned out to prepare for the rest of the evening.

Upstairs in the large tiled bathroom that Papa built for his small army of children, two little girls watched as three of their sisters got ready for the evening.

"Pass me that lipstick," Francesca said to Sophia as she rubbed pink rouge on her cheeks.

"Not until you pass me that rouge," Sophia snapped back.

Francesca had just finished the light-blue chiffon dress she'd sewn by hand. It fit like a glove, showing off her shapely body and matching her eyes. With her perfectly styled dark hair, flawless skin, and impeccable attire, she could easily be mistaken for a Hollywood model. She applied a final coat of lipstick and then twirled around the bathroom, leaving her younger sisters with their mouths open.

"Don't worry," she said to the littlest one before she left the bathroom, "I'll brush your hair and put some ribbons in it before I leave."

The littlest one beamed in delight.

Outside Francesca's home, Buicks, Oldsmobiles, and Ford trucks began to line up on the street. After jostling between the stubborn piles of dirty snow that persisted throughout the Massachusetts town, all were reminded that the cold, harsh winter was finally stepping aside for spring. One by one, anxious boys entered the house through the back door and headed straight into the kitchen, where Mama was still cooking and cleaning.

Mama was a busy woman—proud, strong, and resourceful. She spent her days cooking, gardening, sewing, and lending an ear or a helpful hand to all the people in her life.

Papa, a kind man with a large presence, loved his children dearly, and he took every opportunity to make each feel distinctive and special. After dinner, Papa made his way down to the basement, where he opened a bottle of his homemade wine and poured some into a jelly glass. The boys who lived there were instructed to greet the visiting boys and send them down to the basement, one at a time.

"Sit," Papa said as he slapped the cushion on the seat next to him. "Whatsa you name?"

The targeted boy sat nervously for a few moments until the warmth of Papa's smile put him at ease. After a short conversation that no one was privy to, Papa would decide if the young man passed the "date test." No one would ever know what the consequence would be if Papa handed down a failing grade, because for Papa, the ritual was about the test, not the score.

"Gooda boy," he said as he patted the young man on the back. "Here. You hava nice glassa wine. Ah, thatsa good," Papa said after taking a long sip.

Papa beamed in delight with his rosy cheeks and distinctive gray hair. The nervous boys remained speechless.

Satisfied with their appearances (yet unaware how long their dates had been waiting), the sisters came down the stairs to greet the young men and dash them off to the club for a night of dancing. Heads turned to get a glimpse of Francesca on the dance floor. She was beautiful, fun, and easygoing, and she brought a fullness of life to every party. It was at one of those dances where Francesca met her husband.

"Sophia, do you know that guy over there?" she asked her sister.

"Yes, I work with him. That's Paul."

"Introduce me to him...*please!*"

Paul was a small man with a large personality who fell head over heels for Francesca. Francesca thought he was cute and fun and found herself falling for his charismatic manner. After a year of dating, they married in the fall of 1956, and four children quickly followed. First a daughter, followed by a son eleven months later, and two years after that, twin boys.

I am that daughter.

~

As our family grew in size, Dad found his charming personality preferred to entertain the regulars at the local barroom instead of those of us who waited for him at home. We settled into a house in the same neighborhood where my mother spent her childhood days. The circular street had a total of ten houses, three of which belonged to my aunts and uncles, who filled them with my cousins. Another was owned by my grandmother, who had lived alone since Papa died years earlier. Children played around the neighborhood in alternating groups of genders and ages. There were pots of sauce simmering on stoves, homemade pasta being rolled out on tabletops, kids playing hopscotch and Wiffle ball, and crying babies being rolled down the street in carriages.

"Peggy, tell your mom to come over for a cup of coffee," said Aunt Lou.

"OK, I'll go tell her."

We loved living in our sheltered little world surrounded by family. Grandma loved the short walk for early evening coffee at our kitchen table, something she did every night. The other half of the neighborhood was divided. Three of the families loved being surrounded by this big, loud, loving Italian clan. The other three families hated it.

Daddy used it as an excuse to spend every day at the bar. "It's like being married to seven women. They're always around," he groaned.

Through the years, we came to realize that we preferred it when Daddy wasn't home. Like a chameleon changing colors, we changed our disposition to accommodate his presence—even Mom. Still, underneath his offensive behavior, I could sometimes catch a glimpse of whatever it was that attracted Mom to him.

I cherished the time I spent with my father—before alcohol poisoned his body and corrupted his thoughts. The memory of four sets of shoes, brightly polished and neatly lined up by the back door, was one of them. It meant Mom was preparing to take us to church in the morning. Oh, how I loved the sight of those glossy Mary Janes at the end of the row. All night long, I would think about wearing the blue velvet jacket with the white fur trim, and the hat and muff to match that Nana bought and Mom stored away in the closet for special occasions. It made me feel like Shirley Temple—*rich* and *fancy*. But most of the time, when Sunday morning came, my brothers' shoes stayed by the back door, leaving only Daddy and me to attend Mass. Mom would lose the battle with the boys who didn't want to go and redirect her attention to the only child who was happy to spend an hour in church.

"Stop tickling me," Daddy said as he drove down the street. I sat right next to him, leaving enough room for two more people to join us on the bench seat of the Chevy Impala.

"Daddy, you're tickling *me*," I giggled.

"Don't touch the steering wheel," he said with a laugh.

Following Mass, we would stop at the Italian deli and get a loaf of fresh-baked bread and four little packages of M&M's. The bread never made it to the table; Daddy put it on the counter near the stove, took it out of its wrapper, and placed the bread on top. Like a flock of seagulls, the family would hover around the stove, rip off a piece of bread, dip it in the big pot of bubbly red sauce, eat it with delight, and move out of the way for the next person waiting in line.

Mom gave us the M&M's later that afternoon. Each boy devoured his bag in a matter of minutes, while I took my time with mine. I separated the colors and turned them into artwork: flowers with the tan and red, stems with the green, sunshine with the yellow, and the brown were for eating,

"Mom, the boys are trying to steal my M&M's," I whined as I was jolted out of my moment by an intruding hand or two.

"Boys, you ate yours, now leave your sister's alone," Mom replied back.

They wouldn't have tried to steal any if Daddy was home, I thought. They knew all too well he would jump at the opportunity to belittle them.

Every night around five o'clock, Mom would give the order. "Peggy call your father."

"Awww, why do I always have to do it?" I said. I did as I was told, and I knew exactly where to call. That number was embedded in my brain and will stay there until the day I die.

"Paul, your daughter's on the phone," I heard the bartender say. "He'll be right home," he added.

"OK, thank you." *Darkness was coming home.*

We all worked to stay out of Daddy's path until he inevitably passed out on the couch in front of the only television set, waking only to yell at anyone who dared to change the channel. Every once in a while, when I thought he was asleep, I would tempt fate and change it.

"What the hell are you doing?" he screamed as if I'd just removed one of his limbs.

"I want to watch *Little House on the Prairie*," I said.

"I'm watching the game," he barked.

My brothers and I spent as little time as possible at home during his visiting hours. My mother became two different people. When he was out of the house, she was fun to be around, full of life and love, and relished being in the company of her children and family. But the minute Dad walked through the door, the whole dynamic changed, her smile disappeared and anyone who could leave—did.

〜

While we all mastered the art of maneuvering around Dad's presence, there were times when it was completely unavoidable. That Christmas Eve of 1967 was one of those "memorable" times. My mother took the day off from work. She, my brothers, and I spent the whole day together preparing for Christmas Day. Filled with food, treats, and joy, we kids went to bed feeling loved, safe, and happy. Too soon, we would soon be jolted into the reality of that other side of our childhood.

Daddy's favorite bar closed early on Christmas Eve, so he established a tradition of bringing his "pals" home from the bar to continue celebrating the birth of the baby Jesus at our home. Every year, Mom put her feelings aside to be hospitable. Every year, he pushed the limit by coming home a little later and a little drunker—until the year something inside of Mom finally snapped like a twig in a New England nor'easter.

"Francesca, I'm home!" he yelled as he walked through the door, peacock tail in full bloom.

"Shhhh. The kids are asleep." Mom quickly greeted him and his pals at the door.

"What do you mean shushing me? It's Christmas Eve, for Christ's sake!"

Daddy got out the Christmas albums, pulled one out of its cover, and proceeded to play it.

"Paul, turn that down please." She tried to address her husband in a firm manner, but he didn't notice. He was focused on impressing his friends. "Why don't you make us something to eat?" he demanded.

"Fine, but please turn the music down."

He complied, and Mom headed back to the kitchen, but as soon as she turned the corner, Daddy turned the volume up. No one was going to tell him what to do. No one ever told him what to do, and no one was going to ruin his party. Every time Mom told him to turn the music down, he turned it up until the completely obnoxious level jolted all four sleeping children into an upright position.

"Paul, what are you doing? I told you that music is too loud," Mom said. "Now look what you've done. You woke up the kids."

"Oh, bullshit. You don't know what you're talking about. The kids are up because they're excited about Christmas."

He didn't let up, and I could see Mom trying to hold herself together on the outside while her insides were breaking into little pieces of hurt, frustration, and fury. He had demeaned her many times, but never like that in front of his friends. She liked his friends and their wives and was devastated when she realized he thought so little of her to berate her in such a public forum. Mom took us back to bed, his pals became uncomfortable and left, and the all-too-familiar yelling bellowed out of the living room until Daddy finally passed out.

I thought about *his* mother. Nana, a proper Irish lady, was gentle and sweet, and she would never have approved of his behavior. Nor would his kind Italian father. Unlike Mom's side of the family—chaotic, large, loud, always eating, always working, always playing (often all at the same time), Nana and Gramp's house was orderly, sparse, and quiet. There were no toys, no wine, and scheduled mealtimes, naptimes, bedtimes, and play-times. Was that why he was wild and she was calm?

~

My father took Christmas joy out of my mother's heart that year. The next morning, I saw the hollow of Mom's disengaged face. Her feelings of anger and sadness were not lost on me and reminded me of my own confusing feelings about Christmas Day. The joy of receiving gifts and being with family mixed with the pervasive pain of seeing sadness in my mother's eyes created angst in my little body. That year, my mother had had enough.

The day after Christmas, she placed her four children in the car along with every single Christmas album we had and took us for a ride.

The old blue station wagon drove us up a hill and past the little wood-en sign that read town dump. It chugged us past acres of trees, then onto a dirt road with sand on either side until we got to the top of the hill, where a big hole lay open to accept trash and unwanted treasures. Mom got out of the car, took the pile of Christmas albums with her, and dropped them on the ground.

I jumped out of the car and followed after her. "Mom, please don't throw the records away," I pleaded.

The damage was done. Her mind was made up. I watched in hor-ror as she threw the albums in the dump hole, one by one. *A Classical Christmas* went into the hole, followed by *The Nutcracker*, works by the Philharmonic Orchestra and Elvis, the Lettermen, Frank Sinatra, and oth-ers. They all went into the hole. When I saw *Pepino the Italian Mouse* on the pile, my eyes widened and I had a lump in my throat. "Mom, please, no! Please stop."

"It's too late, Peggy. I'm throwing them out."

But Mom was a kind and reasonable woman. I was sure I could snap her to her senses and make her stop. This just wasn't like her. "I'll tell Daddy not to do it ever again. Please stop!"

She paused to look at me. "Arrrggg!" she screamed as she hurled Pepino off into the hole with all her strength.

When I saw the Chipmunks album in her hand, the lump went down to my stomach, and tears filled my eyes. "Mom, *please!*"

"I told you; it's too late."

"But the Chipmunks? Mom, can we at least keep the Chipmunks—please?"

"No!" she said, and off it went into the hole like a discarded Frisbee.

At least there was one behavior that she could control. There would be no more loud Christmas music for a while. On that day, in that moment, Mom's Christmas joy would be extinguished forever. It was left there in the town dump, in the hole, on top of the pile of abandoned albums.

TWO

*Give your kids all you've got, because once you're done,
you're done.
You can't go back and do it over."*

—Francesca Jean

Mom worked part time outside the home, taking advantage of family baby-
sitters. When all her children were in school full time, she went to work at
a large company as a switchboard operator. She spent her days sitting in
a small room in front of an extensive metal panel filled with numbers. Five
women, sitting arm to arm in a row of chairs with headsets on, plugged
metal connectors into small holes above a number that directed the call
to the requested person. When the call was completed, the plug was
pulled out. When I called her at work, I was prepared to be put on hold at
a moment's notice, often right in the middle of a sentence.

"Hold on," Mom said, unplugging my call to take another. While I
never knew who she would plug me into while completing her work calls,
I knew for sure it wasn't the same kind of conversation other kids had with
their mothers when they were at work.

"New England Company," someone answered.

"Hi, it's Peggy. Can I speak with my mother, please?" I asked.

"Sure, honey, hold on," the woman answered.

While on hold, I had plenty of time to picture what was going on
behind the scenes. The six women who worked in the switchboard office
had families of their own; each had a story to tell. Five worked on the

board, and one was the supervisor who worked at a desk in the same room. Four had children; two did not. The five worked well together, even though one was a troublemaker. Mom worked there for years so I knew them well, except for the troublemaker.

"Hello," Mom said when she finally came on the line.

"Mom, can I skip school tomorrow for senior skip day?"

"Hold on."

Off she went into the black hole, leaving me again with my imagination.

"Where are you?" she asked when she came back on the line.

"I'm home."

"Why do you want to skip school?"

"All the kids are doing it, Mom. Can I, please?"

"Hold on."

I went back to my visual of the women chatting between plugs when suddenly I heard a recording of Father So-and-So giving me a lecture on how to be a good person, determine right from wrong, and follow the path to redemption. I listened to the six-minute lecture that for an impatient teenager, seemed to stretch into hours.

"Do you still want to skip school?" she asked when she came back on the line.

"Yes."

"OK, I'll write the note when I get home. Start dinner, please."

"I will. Thanks, Mom!"

⁓

I didn't mind starting the dinner that Mom always finished when she got home from work. I loved sitting at the small kitchen table with my brothers, listening to them talk about their days. I even got to throw in a joke or two. Mom, who'd walked through the door fifteen minutes earlier, roamed about the kitchen lost in her thoughts, never seeming to hear a word.

"My friend Jimmy got suspended today," my oldest brother Tim said.

"Oh no. What did he do now?" I asked.

Mom stood over the stove with her back to us, eating the stuffing off the top of the pork chops that were spitting grease from the old black cast-iron pan. As Tim explained the circumstances of Jimmy's suspension, I took four crisp, hot, bulky rolls out of the oven and placed one beside each plate at the table while my two younger brothers hung on Tim's every word. Suddenly Mom let out a hearty laugh. We all stopped to look at her, but she didn't even seem to notice we were in the same room.

"What's so funny, Mom?" I asked.

"Oh, I was just thinking about something that happened at work to-day," she replied.

Tim, who lost interest in telling Jimmy's story, stood up and stared at the beautiful, full, round rolls. He made a fist—and as if playing a game of Whack-a-Mole—smashed each hot roll into the table with four swift blows. Mom, who was still by the stove, was oblivious to her children's actions. As long as we were safe and happy, Mom didn't intervene. It fed my soul when we were all together, laughing, eating, sharing, and happy. Dad, on the other hand, who only joined us at the dinner table a couple of times a month, did not make the dinner experience fun or happy. No one spoke, there were no jokes, no smashed rolls, no misbehaving, and very little eating, yet Dad would always manage to find something to yell about. Dad yelled when he had no reason to. Mom giggled when she could have been yelling.

~

The most significant call I made to my mother while she was at work would be the last time I ever called the New England Company.

"New England Company," she answered.

I had been working on my wedding plans for months, and my fiancé's parents were fighting me every step of the way. It was so distressing I had to see a doctor, who wrote me a prescription for something to settle my stomach, which was constantly in knots.

"Tom's parents won't sign the papers indicating he's never been married," I said through tears.

"What do you mean, they won't sign?" she asked

"They won't sign. His mother doesn't want him to marry me," I wailed.

"Hold on."

While I was on hold a lot longer than the usual hold time, I thought about the troublemaker. *She must be just like my soon-to-be mother-in-law*, I thought. *Unhappy people don't like it when anyone else is happy.*

"Peggy, I just put you on hold for the very last time."

"What do you mean, Mom?"

"I quit work."

"What?"

"I've been unplugging you long enough. I'm not doing it anymore."

"Wow. Mom?"

I couldn't believe she actually did something for herself. She spent her whole life doing things for others. She worked from the time she got up in the morning until her head hit the pillow at night. On weekends, she scrubbed the house. She didn't take time at a spa, no one took her out to dinner, and she never sat down to read a book. Her happiness came from her children, her merriment came from family events large and small, and her relaxation came when she was sick. Every day after she left work, she stopped at the grocery store to buy rolls and lunch meat for the next day, and when she came through the door, she found her mother sitting at the kitchen table. She'd then put a pot of coffee on the stove and run to the opposite end of the house to her bedroom to change out of her work clothes.

"Francesca, the coffee's boiling over!" Grandma yelled from her seat at the kitchen table as the coffee splashed onto the electric burner.

"I'll get it, Mom," I said, loud enough for her to hear out of the kitchen, through the living room, and into the bathroom off the side of her bedroom.

Mom poured two cups of coffee and tended to dinner while Grandma worked on her crocheting. They chatted for a few hours, and when

Grandma left, Mom prepped for the next day. She did laundry, made lunches, and got her work clothes ready. That was Mom's day, every Monday through Friday.

~

Mom was kind to anyone and everyone who sat at her kitchen table, and her children's friends were happy to spend time there. She welcomed every one of my boyfriends and trusted me to behave while spending alone time with them. She looked beyond their long hair and strange smells. She gave me leeway with curfews on special occasions. Dad wasn't around for the meet-and-greets, but when he did get a glimpse of a boy I liked, he always found something wrong with him. I thought that was what all dads did.

After high school, I took a job at a local silver factory while still living at home. One day I came home from work to see Mom and Auntie Cathy sitting at the kitchen table. They both looked very somber, and I immediately knew that something was wrong. A hush fell over them as they quickly changed the subject before Auntie Cathy got up to leave a few minutes later. Mom had learned that my latest boyfriend, Kyle, with whom I had been dating for two years, wanted to get married. Kyle talked about it all the time, but I managed to put him off until he got really mad one night and challenged me to a bet. If he won, we had to set a date for our wedding, a wedding I had no interest in planning or even attending, for that matter. He won the bet, and we set the date for May. Somehow Auntie Cathy heard the news and relayed it to Mom.

"Peggy, what are you doing?" Mom asked. "You're not ready for marriage. He doesn't even have a decent job."

"He's the one who wants to get married," I explained.

Her voice raised and her body arched like she'd been hit in the back by something big and hard. She didn't appear to be angry, just concerned and desperate.

"If you marry him, you're going to end up in a third-floor apartment with three kids and no washer and dryer," she said.

She was flustered, but she wasn't yelling—she was pained, but not *in* pain. I didn't understand the urgency in her voice, so I continued to listen, still processing this odd scene.

What's the big deal? I thought. My young mind thought it might be kind of fun to be engaged.

"I have an idea," Mom proposed. "I spoke with Auntie Mae, and you can go live there and work at her restaurant." Auntie Mae owned a restaurant that was once an inn, so it had many little hotel rooms upstairs, as well as a kitchen and living area. She lived in the living area with her family and housed employees and family members in the remaining rooms.

I stood quietly and listened.

"Peggy, you're so young. You don't even know what's out there yet. You don't have to settle down now."

I was speechless. I didn't understand what all the fuss was about. I didn't even want to marry Kyle.

"Go stay with Auntie Mae. If you two really love each other, a few months apart won't destroy your relationship. Go spend the summer away, and if you still want to get married in the fall, I'll support you."

"But *live* there?" I asked.

"You're only forty minutes away. You'll be fine."

My mother loved me with all her heart, and I knew how important her proposal was, so I agreed. As monumental as it was for her, it was equally as inconsequential to me. Six months after graduating high school, I moved away from home to work for Auntie Mae. Like a psychic with a mission, she accomplished her goal. Weeks after freedom from Kyle and the monotony of my hometown, I met new people, went out on dates, worked, played, and forgot all about marriage for over a year until Tom came into my life.

~

I met Tom on a blind date while working at Auntie Mae's restaurant. His childhood friend Ben was working at the restaurant and staying in one of the rooms upstairs. Ben was determined to find the perfect match for Tom, and after many attempts, he was on notice—this was his last chance. Some girls fall in love with men who remind them of their fathers, I fell for one who was the complete opposite. When he walked through the door to greet me, I knew that image would stay with me forever. He wore a white turtleneck, blue jeans, and hand-stitched cowboy boots that made him seem as tall as the Jefferson Monument.

"Hello," he said, towering over me by a foot. "Ready to go?"

He spoke about things I had never experienced, and I wanted to listen to him forever. His father's job was with an airline, and Tom was a sailor, so like his father, he had traveled all over the world. I was completely captivated when he talked about the stars, their names and constellations. Tom introduced me to the world above me that I never really noticed. A gentleman and a protector, he opened doors for me and never let me walk on the outside of the sidewalk. He was polite and respectful, and he asked permission for that first kiss instead of just taking it. He was soft, kind, and generous. On one of our earliest dates, he stopped at a small convenience store.

"OK, little one, I'll just be a minute. Can I get you anything?" he asked.

"Yes, please, I'll take some Life Savers."

"What kind would you like?"

"Surprise me."

He came out of the store, opened the car door, and placed a little brown paper bag in my lap. I opened it up and found ten rolls of Life Savers inside.

"That's one of every variety they had," he said.

I stopped breathing for a moment. Whirlpools of thoughts spun around in my head, trying to recall a time when any of my other dates demonstrated such a kind gesture.

He was in awe at how naïve I was and delighted in presenting me with new experiences. On our first formal dinner date, he took me to a French restaurant, reserved a special table, and ordered wine.

"We'll have the Chateaubriand for two," he said to the waiter.

"What's that?" I asked.

"Trust me. You'll love it."

I did. I loved how he looked at me. I loved everything about him.

He passed the acceptance test with my mother because he made me happy. He passed my father's test by bringing him a six-pack of Schlitz the first time they met. He passed the uncle test (an important test to pass in an Italian family) by giving them his time and attention. And he passed the brother test by letting them borrow his sports car. He was spontaneous, fun, and more than a little mischievous. And he had a great job (albeit on a ship that took him away for months at a time). Still, he was perfect.

On our way out to dinner in June 1977, he pulled into a scenic area under a bridge and parked the car. The fullness of the moon revealed an uneasiness on his face. He sat there pensively for a long time.

"What's going on?" I asked.

"I'm afraid," he said.

"What are you afraid of?"

"I'm afraid you won't marry me."

"Well, ask. Why do you think I won't marry you?"

We sat and negotiated the terms of our marriage. I didn't want to raise a family with a husband who would be home for three months then gone for four. Four months with very little communication and no interaction. No cell phones, no e-mail, no Skype. No hugs, no words of praise, no positive role-modeling for my children to witness on a regular basis. My children would have an active father, a good father. That lifestyle worked for some families, and the pay was lucrative, but for me, it just wasn't worth the sacrifice. He wanted to ship out until he accomplished his goal of earning the highest license.

"We won't have children for at least two years while I ship out and work toward becoming captain. And then I'll look for a shore job," he concluded.

"That's fair," I agreed.

We set the date for the next spring, while his friends took bets on how long the marriage would last.

As smitten as my family was with Tom, his family had other thoughts about me. Only twenty years old, they said, I was too young, uneducated, Italian, Catholic, and lived in a Democratic state! While Tom and I dated that first year, they tolerated me and remained pleasant when we were together, but their true feelings became quite clear on the day he gathered them all together in the formal living room to announce our engagement.

"Peggy and I are getting married," he said to his mother, father, sister, and brother.

The smile on my face quickly vanished as I heard the comments coming from the small audience in front of me.

"*What?*"

"What do you mean?"

"But you're just dating. It's not the real thing."

"You can't marry her."

"What about Darlene? She's perfect for you."

"What about Courtney? She comes from a nice Irish family. She darns socks."

Suddenly, his mother got up and dragged him off into the kitchen. His father followed.

His sister and brother broke off and went into the family room.

I sat in a chair in that living room all by myself...for a very long time.

"What the hell is going on here?" I whispered to no one.

My mind went blank as I searched for a pathway that would enlighten me. My head was frozen in place while my eyes moved left to right as if watching a tennis match.

Have I ever been alone in a living room before—anywhere, ever? I thought. *Yes, at night, when you babysat and all the kids had gone to bed. And you hated it*, I answered myself in my head.

"Don't make me choose," I heard Tom say to his mother from the kitchen.

"Tommy, I just—"

"Ma, you won't like the answer."

I don't remember how or when I made my exit.

The only family member who was supportive about the union was his brother, who was away in the air force. But I wouldn't find that out until a week later when his letter arrived, welcoming me to the family.

Later that evening, while safely in his arms, I finally emerged from the fog that safeguarded me from that antagonistic meeting. "Courtney darns socks?" I asked.

"A life filled with old socks and no love. But hey, a happy mother," he half-joked.

It took years before I realized that my mother-in-law Margaret Mary Murphy's attitude was less about me and more about losing her child to another. After her other two sons married and countless "keep peace" talks from my mother, we became great friends. I won my father-in-law over years earlier when he'd barked at me in the kitchen and I barked right back.

"That's not the way it's done," he ordered.

"That's the way I do it," I snapped back.

He looked at me intensely and said, "I like you. You've got spunk."

"I like you too," I said in relief and gave him a peck on the cheek.

THREE

My True Love

TOM AND I got married and moved two states away from my sheltered neighborhood and into the home he purchased from his grandparents, who lived right next door to my in-laws. We had two babies within the first two years of marriage.

"Mom, I don't understand. How can I be pregnant again?"

"It just happens that way for some people," she replied.

"But he was only home for a short time."

"That's the way it goes."

"But—"

"Peggy, if you don't know by now, you better buy a book!"

I knew. I was hoping the rant would ease the pain of breaking the deal we negotiated under the bridge, not once but twice.

Tom shipped out full time for the first three years of our married life, until he became captain. When he was away, the isolation was unbearable. His parents all but shunned me for not following the rules they assumed I learned through osmosis, so I packed up the kids and made the three-hour drive to temporarily move in with Mom.

"I hate it when he leaves," I told her. "And this kid is going to be the death of me," I added, referring to my oldest son.

John was an overly active child. He figured out how to get out of his crib at eight months old, never to return again. He learned to walk long before he was a year old and immediately started exploring. Everything interested him—everything except toys. He removed every book from bookcases and every pan out of cupboards, munched on plants, found his way beyond anything baby-proofed (and all but took a bow afterward). He was my little Houdini, and I couldn't take my eyes off him for one single minute.

"Those kinds of kids make interesting adults," Mom said daily to ease my frustration.

"Great, Mom," I replied, "but that doesn't make it any easier now."

"I'll watch the kids. Why don't you get out of the house?"

"I don't know. I feel so frumpy."

"Get out of those maternity pants and go put some jeans on."

I rolled my eyes.

"Go."

I did as I was told and came back into the kitchen with my jeans unzipped and opened.

"See," I said in a huff. "They don't fit."

"Come over here." She pulled the jeans up to my waist the same way she did when I was a lot younger. The wistful memory of being her little girl made my heart swirl. We were equals now, and I wondered how long it would be before I was the one pulling her pants up to her waist.

"Now suck that belly in," she demanded.

She buttoned the top button, zipped up the fly, and stood back to inspect me.

"There. You look great. Now go on out and have some fun."

~

Unable to take her own "fun" advice, Mom stayed married to Dad for the boys.

"What does he do for the boys?" I asked.

"Not much, but if they act up in school, he goes in and straightens it out."

When the twins went off to college, my parents decided to sell our family home and rent an apartment just a block off the bustling main street in a town much closer to my family. Tom had left his seagoing job months earlier, and we relocated to a small New England town, where he took a shoreside position. Mom found a new job and new friends and reunited with a favorite niece and her friends—and together they made that Main Street their own. She and Dad settled into a roommate relationship. They kept different hours, ran in different circles, and coexisted only on weekend days. She was able to see her grandchildren at least twice a week, and I loved having her nearby. Every couple of months, I left the kids home with Tom so I could spend the night with her. We strolled Main Street, talked for hours, laughed loudly, swapped stories, and counseled and consoled each other.

"Why don't you leave him, Mom?" I asked.

"Where would I go?" she answered.

"Mom, you're young, you're beautiful, and unless you leave him, you'll never know what it's like to have a meaningful conversation with a man you really like."

"I know," she acquiesced. But she really didn't know. She went from her home with her mother to her home with my father. I felt sad that I was experiencing something she had not. "Don't you want to go out to a nice dinner and share a bottle of wine with someone pleasant who will listen to you? All Dad wants to do is argue."

"Yes! But what am I going to do? It's not like I can move in with my mother."

"Come live with me."

"I couldn't."

"Yes, you could. Mom," I said. "We would love to have you."

⁓

Mom moved from the apartment she shared with Dad to our home in May 1984. After many years of being subjected to my father's appalling behavior, she was beyond weary. On the day he gambled away the rent money for the third month in a row, she had no choice. They were evicted, and she had no place to go. I was thrilled to see her get out of an un-healthy relationship. As happy as I was to have her come live with us, I was completely unprepared for the impact this new facet would have on our already demanding household. Tom and I had been married for six years, and we had three young children: John, five years; Daniel, four years; and Matthew, six weeks old.

"Tom, do you have anyone to help you move Mom?" I asked.

"No. Once again, your brothers are all busy," he replied.

"I can't help. I have to work today. I told Auntie Mae I would waitress. Mother's Day is the busiest day of the year."

Tom and Mom made the move together, making multiple trips from her old home to her new home while my father sat on their couch and watched. I'm sure a piece of his heart was breaking, but he was never one to dig deep and express his feelings, so who would know? Mom shared a room with the baby.

"Mom, I'm sorry; I know it's tight in here. You can actually reach out from your bed and rub Matthew's back in his crib," I said.

"I don't mind. It's nice to be able to help out," she replied.

"He'll be in a bed before you know it, and then we'll move him in with his brothers."

The children were young and easily adjusted to the addition of another member to the family. But the transition would be more difficult for the three adults, particularly me. I can't exactly pinpoint what caused me to spiral into depression. The house? The kids? The challenges of balanc-ing a relationship with my husband, my mother, and my children? The stress of dealing with my father, who was lost and popped in for visits while my mother planned her escape? Maybe it was all of the above; I don't know. The emotional mass overpowered me; I became completely impaired and dealt with the situation by spending an entire week in bed. I told myself I was sick, but I knew better—and that's when I started my first love affair with therapy.

"What do you need therapy for?" Tom asked.

"I'm overwhelmed, and I need help," I replied.

"What are you going to talk about?" asked Mom.

"Is it about us?" they both inquired. Mom saw it as a sign of weakness. She believed things were best left unsaid. "I don't understand what you need a therapist for."

"It's all about me," I told them over and over. "I just need some help."

My emotions were running wild.

Excitement got me there twenty-five minutes early.

Anxiety had me so paralyzed I worried I wouldn't be able to get out of the car.

Doubt made me worry that someone passing by would recognize and judge me.

Fear made me question the therapist's character.

What if he's mean?

What if he yells at me?

What if he tells me I'm overreacting?

What if he tells me I'm beyond help?

As I sat in my car, I thought about going home and dealing with my problems alone as Tom and Mom had suggested, but the thought of either one of them saying "I told you so" gave me the strength I needed. I walked into the old building, up the stairs, and into a tiny waiting room to contemplate this new experience for a few minutes before the door opened and someone came out. I buried my head inside a magazine until he left the little room.

A few minutes later, the door opened again. "Hello, Peggy. Come on in."

The inside office was large, and the massive old windows provided lots of light. A tree in a planter caught my eye and directed my sight to a small area with children's books and toys, putting me at ease. *If a kid can do this, so can I*, I thought. Dr. Smith welcomed me and offered me a seat by the window. He was soft-spoken, kind, and mild-mannered and wore navy corduroy slacks with a white button-down shirt and a thin, dark-green sweater. He sat across from me, crossed his legs, gazed at me quietly for a few moments, and then smiled. I was reminded of Mr. Rogers, the character my children watched on public television.

"So, Peggy, tell me about yourself," he said.

"I don't know what's wrong. I can't seem to get out of my own way," I answered.

He nodded and smiled. "I'd like to know about you. We'll get to all that later. Tell me about yourself."

"Me?"

"Yes. You."

"I'm married. I have three kids—all boys—and my mother just moved in with me."

"But what about you? What do you like to do?"

"Me?"

"Yes. Tell me about Peggy outside of being a mother, wife, and daughter."

"Oh." I hadn't thought of myself as anything *but* a wife, mother, and daughter. I never gave myself credit for volunteer, friend, counselor, student, employee, gardener, artist, or writer.

My metaphor for that first year of therapy was "piles of stuff everywhere." I felt like I had stacks of paper six feet high all over the house, each one representing a chore, an emotion, or an issue that I just couldn't complete or resolve. My kind and gentle therapist and I tackled one pile per session. I was completely captivated by this tender man. He was the father I always wanted, the opposite of the one I had. We talked about how to balance relationships and how to unearth and improve organizational skills that seemed to temporarily slip away. It took about a year for my metaphorical piles to dissipate, but when they did, I was much stronger, wiser, and ready for the next phase of life.

Life went on, with Tom and Mom busy in the workforce and me in the home. Therapy provided an opportunity for friendships to build between us as we each learned to vocalize our needs and respect each other's space. Mom was happy to run around after her three little grandchildren when Tom and I needed to escape the busy family, and I treasured the extra pair of hands as well as her wisdom and advice on life. Now single, she was still young and beautiful and had endless energy and enough laughter to fill the hearts of everyone she met. She worked full time and was able to enjoy outings with family and friends.

Tom and Mom quickly learned that laughter was the key to breaking through any tense situation. One night when I was overwhelmed with housework, Tom jumped in to help out with the laundry. He took the clean clothes out of the dryer, put them in the basket, and brought them to the room where my mother and I were sitting. He took out a pair of skimpy black lace underwear and held them up like he was trying to sell them on QVC. "These are my mother-in-law's," he joked to his audience of two. He then picked up the granny panties and held them up. "And these are my wife's."

He continued to take out pieces of clothing and held up a shiny black nightgown. "This is my mother-in-law's," he said and quickly replaced it with a baggy pair of sweatpants. "And these are my wife's."

Tom's unwavering good humor became a peacemaking tool that carried over onto our children. Throughout our marriage, he was the family mediator who quietly and constantly worked to keep everyone happy and in harmony with his family.

Mom was happy to purchase new pajamas for the kids and, every once in a while, a new gift for the home. One evening after work, she met up with her friend. The two of them went shopping and then had dinner and a glass of wine. Tom and I had just gone to bed when she came through the door, high heels clomping, giggling to herself as she roamed around to and fro instead of her usual routine of quietly heading to her bedroom.

"What's with your mother? What is she doing?" Tom asked.

"I don't know. She'll go to bed in a minute," I replied.

Vrroooommmmmm!

A machine suddenly roared from the kitchen, followed by peals of laughter from Mom.

"What the hell is that?" Tom snorted.

"I don't know, Tom. Just give her a minute."

Vrroooommmmmm!

The machine roared proudly a second time, and Mom broadcast her delight with another long giggle.

"Peggy, seriously what is she doing? I'm trying to go to sleep."

"She went to the mall after work. I think she bought a coffee grinder. Just give her another minute. She'll go to bed."

Vrrooooommmmmmm!

With that, Tom had had enough. "Francesca!" he yelled. "Take your new toy upstairs. I'm trying to get some sleep."

Mom's giggle turned into hearty laughter as she clomped and cackled all the way up the stairs to her bedroom. Tom shook his head in bewilderment, and his annoyed expression transformed into a toothy grin.

"Your mother is crazy," he said softly. Little did I know that five-letter term of endearment would soon become a politically incorrect word that would somehow take over my life.

As I drifted off to sleep, I wondered about that word. *Crazy.* How many times had I been called crazy or called others crazy? I wondered about people who exhibited irrational behavior, and I wrestled with the crossover line until my thoughts became one big blur.

~

For the next four years, our home ran like a well-rehearsed play. We demonstrated kindness, established boundaries, and celebrated respect for each other. We laughed together and felt each other's pain. We marched in rhythm to the beat of our home, right up to the day we decided to build a new house—one with a huge kitchen, a small private suite for us, a small private suite for Mom, and more room for our growing boys. But building the house put a dangerous strain on our family. On top of the typical issues of the build taking months longer than initially predicted and costing thousands more than originally quoted, the contractor, our dear friend Sam, left town before completing the job. He was fighting his own demons and just picked up and left one day, leaving behind two emotionally devastated and financially drained families. Suddenly Tom found himself finishing the house on his own while working a full-time job, with a very small financial reserve, a nagging wife, and three ambitious boys. We thanked our lucky stars for the students we hired. We paid them a practical wage, fed them, and played their music, and they had some fun while working with their friends. They finished floors, walls, closets, and the kitchen. They painted, sanded, cut wood, and nailed. They landscaped and washed windows. They saved our asses! And they did it while three little boys were helping.

"Where's the tape measure?" one student asked.

"Look in the back of Matthew's truck," Tom replied.

At five years old, Matthew took pride in helping with each task. He rode everywhere on his little plastic truck, checking on jobs inside and out.

"Peggy, where is the paperwork for the appliances?" Tom asked.

"Look in Matthew's briefcase," I yelled from another room.

The process was slow. While the house was being put together piece by piece, Tom and I were falling apart. Our strained relationship took a turn down an unkind, nasty road. "When are you going to finish this house?" I said.

"When are you going to get a real job instead of just working when the spirit moves you?" he said.

"When are *you* going to make more money?" I said.

"When are you going to get off my back?" he said. "I work all day and come home to help you do what you should've had done already. Then I have to go work on the house."

We were both dealing with the same painful situation, but we weren't dealing with it together. We drank because we were stressed, and then we fought because we were drunk. We were finding satisfaction from tearing each other down instead of leaning on each other for comfort. Our brains were foggy, our emotions were raw, our fighting was intense, and the sex was sizzling hot—but it was all destructive and exhausting.

We traveled down that disrespectful road for almost a year until it came to an abrupt stop while on a family vacation. We were all in the same hotel room when the fighting became impossible to hide. Nine-year-old Daniel sat up and stared at us.

"Do you two realize what you sound like?" Daniel asked calmly.

Daniel was bright beyond his years; even at that young age, he was a writer and an artist. He read everything from children's books to Shakespeare. He loved words, and that night, his words were powerful. Tom and I just stared at him and then at each other.

"I'm sorry, Daniel," I said.

"We'll stop. Go back to sleep," Tom replied.

Tom and I had discussed this very issue before we had children. We each watched our parents fight and insult each other throughout their marriages. We didn't want our children to live in that environment.

"I didn't know they heard us fighting," I said.

"Of course they do. How could they not know what's going on?"

And that's when I had my second love affair with therapy. My sweet therapist became *our* sweet therapist. He saw each of us individually for a few months before bringing us together as a couple.

"Here we are. Are you two ready to go forward?" Dr. Smith said.

"Yes," we replied in unison.

"I know you love each other. I think you each lost sight of that."

Dr. Smith spoke for a while, and then he looked at me. Without a word, he cautioned me. *It was time to give Tom a voice.*

"I don't feel like I have any say on what goes on in the house," Tom said.

"What do you mean?" I asked.

"For example, I never liked the kitchen tables the way they are. I think they should be switched around."

"Kitchen tables?" I said. "Is this really about kitchen tables, Tom?"

"Peggy, listen," Dr. Smith said kindly but firmly.

"Yes. You never even asked me what I thought about the kitchen tables. You just did what you wanted to do."

"We can change the kitchen tables."

"Good," he said in triumph.

Kitchen tables? I thought. *We almost got a divorce over kitchen tables?*

Our kitchen had two big tables—one for meals and one for homework. Tom built one of the tables when we were first married, picking the top up at a yard sale, building the legs, and cutting out a large heart on each end of the trestle. We used that table for supervising homework. The homework table was neat and tidy for one day every couple of months when we had guests for a holiday or party, but otherwise, it was continuously cluttered with books, papers, and ongoing assignments. John spent the most time sitting at that table. For every minute he spent doing homework, he spent ten dreaming about the future or thinking about how he could help other people. "When I get married, I'm going to adopt a kid from every country," he said in a strong, proud voice.

"Wow, that's a lot of kids," I replied.

"Maybe not from *every* country."

"Then you better get your homework done. You're going to have to get a good job to feed all those kids."

"I want to be a teacher."

That's admirable, but you won't make much money, I thought.

"That's nice. You'll be a great teacher," I agreed out loud. "What about social work, John? Have you ever thought about doing that work?"

"And how is that going to help the children of the world?"

"Kids need counseling. You do it all the time, and you don't even know it."

"No. I want to work in the public school system."

"OK," I said and finished loading the dishwasher.

Daniel rarely sat at the homework table. He was self-motivated and got all his homework done upstairs in his room, in pen, with rarely an error and very little prompting. Many of his teachers told us he was gifted and we should send him to a private school, where he could be challenged academically, but Tom and I believed all three boys were gifted in their own way, and it wouldn't be right to separate one out of the mix. Besides, we didn't have the money after building a new house.

Matthew spent a variable amount of time at the homework table, mostly doing homework. He wasn't trustworthy enough to do the work on his own, but when told to get it done, he didn't waste any time. But being the baby of the family had its benefits. Matthew came and went without the same notice and scrutiny his older brothers received.

John liked sitting in his seat at the head of the table, holding court with the comings and goings of the house. He was less interested in TV, games, and gadgets, and more interested in people. Years later, after receiving his master's degree, he returned to the table to study for his teaching certificate.

"You're on your own, John. Dad and I are going to bed. Shut the lights off when you're done studying," I ordered.

"No prob," he acknowledged.

Tom and I were almost to the bedroom when he yelled, "I'm up to the Civil War."

I smiled as I thought, *If I only had a nickel for every hour that child sat in that chair.*

~

That second love affair with therapy gave me a great gift—the gift of *listening* to my loved ones. After months of marriage therapy, we agreed that it was time to let the past go so we could move forward with a new relationship, one that was built on respect and communication. Soon thereafter, I realized I had never asked Tom about my mother moving in. We discussed it when she had nowhere to go, so of course, he would say it was a good idea. But I didn't give him an opportunity to express his true feelings. I didn't give him a voice and a role in the decision. He walked a fine line of respecting my decisions (because he left me to make many of them alone while he was away) and feeling left out (because I continued to make them alone while he was home). It wasn't about the placement of the kitchen tables at all. The kitchen table was his metaphor for all the decisions made without his input.

I also learned to truly listen to my children. Family dinners at the old homework table, now the kitchen table, became of utmost importance. It was a time for each of us to talk about what was going on in our lives. After realizing that a nine-year-old child had far more composure and perception than both his adult parents put together, I never dismissed anything my children had to say. We didn't always agree, and sometimes their perspectives were very wrong, but I never dismissed their thoughts or belittled them for having them. We learned together—all of us.

~

"I'm going to Florida," my mother announced at the kitchen table one evening.

"Who are you going to visit?" I asked.

"I've rented a condo for the winter."

"What? Why didn't you say anything?"

"Well, I had to make some arrangements at work, and I didn't want to say anything until I had it all figured out."

"What do you mean? When did you decide to do that?"

"You guys have had your hands full lately, and you don't need me around to complicate things."

"But Mom, I do need you."

"You'll be fine without me for a few months, Peggy. Besides, I need to get away."

"Are you going to drive?"

"Yes."

"By yourself? But...but why?"

"I hate the cold, and I want to see what it's like to live there in the winter. My friend Jocelyn is there, and she's looking forward to having me around."

"But—"

"Good for you, Francesca," Tom chimed in.

"Yeah, good for you, Nonni," the boys added.

"I'll come to visit you, Nonni," said Matthew.

"But, Mom!" I mumbled quietly.

My mother needed to get away. After all, she was fifty-five years old; it was time to overcome her fears and find some happiness separate from our family. All her life, she'd let her fears hold her back from doing things that enticed her. Spending the winter in the warmth of Florida was something she wanted badly. It was time to conquer her fears—at least some of them. She was afraid of water, tunnels, bridges, driving alone, being alone, and nighttime. So many things had a way of presenting themselves to my mother as another opportunity for danger or disaster. Throughout the years, in true grandmotherly fashion, she offered protective words of wisdom to her grandchildren, warning them against the multitude of dangers the world has to offer.

"Don't leave a knife on the counter. Someone could come in and hurt you with it."

"Don't sit in front of a window during a thunderstorm. I know a girl who got struck by lightning."

"Don't put your hand out of a car window while driving. I know a girl who lost her arm doing that."

"Don't get too close to a dog. I know a girl who had her nose bit off while kissing a poodle."

"Don't dive into water. I know a girl who broke her neck doing that."

"Don't get on a motorcycle. I know a girl who has brain damage from a motorcycle accident."

"Don't jump in puddles. I know a girl who got ringworm from a puddle."

"Geez, Nonni, that poor girl must be in really rough shape," the boys finally replied in frustration.

"It didn't all happen to the same person," she said. "I'm telling you, it's all true," she added with an enthusiastic giggle.

The next morning, she put her fears aside and drove out of the driveway in her little yellow Mustang, destined for Florida.

FOUR

Murder in the Mustang

Mom was an integral part of our family, and my children adored her. She sang along to their music, laughed at their jokes, and was extremely proud of all their accomplishments—large and small. She mended their clothes, ironed their shirts, and drove them to visit friends. Her involvement with her grandchildren overflowed onto their friends, each of whom called her Nonni.

Mom loved her new life as a snowbird, spending summers in New England and winters in Florida. She had oodles of great people surrounding her in each location. She worked hard through the week and played every weekend. Her favorite Florida gathering place was Panama Jeans. One evening, Daniel called her up and disguised his voice.

"Hello," said Mom in her happy voice.

"Is this Francesca?" he inquired.

"Yes."

"You have just won a twenty-five-dollar gift certificate to Panama Jeans," Daniel said in a deep voice.

She screamed so loudly with excitement he had to pull the phone away from his ear. The laughter far exceeded the disappointment she felt for a second when she realized it was a joke. Her heart was open, loving, happy, and kind. She found her independence, and it showed. She was full of joy and a ton of fun for anyone who had the pleasure of her company.

All her life, my mother has been beautiful, loving, attractive, caring, and healthy. She was also always perfectly presented, impeccably dressed, and she treated herself to blonde highlights and a French pedicure. When she dressed up, she looked like Jackie O. When she dressed down, her favorite attire was a razorback tank top, Daisy Dukes, and fashionable flip-flops with a high wedge. She had a way about her that came across as a little ditsy, although she was a very bright woman. She was extremely self-sufficient. She was the one with the toolbox. She was the one doing the landscaping, carpooling, cooking, cleaning, and raising four kids while working full time. My father did very little to help her around the house, and yet she rarely complained. Now that she was away from him and living half the year with her three wonderful young grandsons and the other half totally independent in Florida, it was as if she had become young again. She was always content and often quirky.

Everyone has their quirks. Quirkiness is a silly, usually harmless trait, but my mother liked to involve others into her quirky world, especially Tom and me.

"Well, seeing as you're going to the store, would you pick me up a lottery ticket?" she asked Tom, even though he had no intention or had given any indication that he was going anywhere at all.

"Oh, and would you stop by the post office and check my mail?"

"OK, Francesca. When I go out," Tom agreed.

"And don't go to that store right down the street," she would insist. "It doesn't know how to hand out winning tickets."

Mom and I had an unspoken agreement. While up north, I did the leading, she did the following; in Florida, the opposite was the case. I always drove up north, she always drove down south. And when it came to parking a car, my mother was quirky. She would drive around every parking lot looking for the best spot, but unlike most people, the "best" spot wasn't the closest to the door. You couldn't park too close to your destination, she believed. "The walk is great exercise." On the other hand, you shouldn't park too far away either. "You could be snatched up by a stranger." For Mom, the end spot was a favorite (unless, of course, it was next to a curb, bush, van, or truck).

In our northern home, all towels were treated equally, but Mom had a different set of rules for her Florida towels. Towels used for drying yourself off after a shower were to be folded and hung on a towel rack inside the shower. Pool towels were to be hung on a clothes hanger in the bedroom closet. Washcloths were completely frowned upon, but on the rare occasion you really needed to use one, it was to be draped over the tub until it dried a bit and then transferred onto a clothes hanger and hung in the closet with the pool towels until it was completely dry and could safely be thrown in the dirty-clothes basket. Beach towels weren't allowed in the house at all. They stayed in the trunk of the car until it was time to wash them, and then they were promptly returned to the trunk.

You couldn't sit outside in the rain, even though there was a roof over your head. You had to be in the house when the sun went down (because that's when bad things started happening in the world). And when she prepared the place for a long absence in the spring, she put plastic wrap over the toilet with a handwritten sign that said "out of order."

"Is that so a burglar won't use the toilet when you're not here?" I asked.

"You never know," she professed confidently.

"Quirky" makes us unique and separates us from the rest of the world. But I began to have concerns when I couldn't distinguish between my mother's customary quirky behavior and her increasingly altered personality. It became extremely difficult to determine what was true, what was exaggerated, and what was completely made up. While sorting through the possible reasons for my mother's fluctuating behavior, one thing I knew for sure: September 11, 2001 changed her forever. She was sixty-seven years old.

As the news of 9/11 surrounded us all day, every day, Mom watched the broadcast 24-7 and began to be suspicious of everyone around her. Her quirky actions and fearful thoughts spun out of control and entered the realm of paranoia. We were together constantly, yet she had entirely different perceptions of what transpired throughout the day.

"I'm going to the grocery store, Mom. Want to come?"

We shopped together until she left me to go to the restroom and pick up some bread. She joined me in the frozen-food aisle, the last stop before checkout. She was quiet in the car on the drive home, so I sang along with the song on the radio. Suddenly she broke her silence.

"Peggy, did you see that man putting poison in the meat at the grocery store?"

"What man?" I asked.

"In the store just now. I saw a man putting poison in the meat."

"What are you talking about?"

I searched my thoughts. If it was something she saw when we were together, I didn't see it. If it was something she saw when we were apart, how could she expect I knew what she was referring to? I sent my mind back to the store and looked at the far end of the supermarket where the meat resided, but I saw nothing out of the ordinary. My mind's eye continued looking up and down the aisles and saw a few familiar bodies pushing carts, but nothing unusual. I finished my search at the front of the store, where a dozen or so cashiers were busy checking people out. Finally, I saw Mom and me having a conversation while we waited our turn and wondered why she hadn't said anything to me then.

"No, Mom. I didn't see anything like that at all."

"They're trying to kill us, you know."

"Who?"

"They are."

"Mom, that's just not true." I hoped my response would bring her back to her senses. We drove in silence for a few moments, and when I thought her fears were put to rest, I turned the radio up and resumed my singing.

"Look at that car over there. Why is it on the side of the road?" she asked moments later.

38

I turned the radio back down. "I don't know; maybe they're visiting someone."

"I bet there's a bomb under it."

"Bomb?"

"Yes, it's all over the news. We're supposed to be watching for terrorists."

She somehow managed to make enough sense to keep the conversation plausible and me engaging in it.

"I know, Mom, but I don't think there's a bomb under that particular car."

"There is."

"How do you know?"

"Peggy, they are dispersing poison through the air. They are putting poison in all the reservoirs. They are putting bombs under all the cars. They are trying to kill us." Her voice was getting louder and more confident.

"Mom, it's not happening here. It's not happening anywhere," I whispered, trying to calm her.

"Peggy, it is too!"

"You can't just say those things unless you know it's happening for sure," I said with my voice rising.

"It *is*," she replied angrily.

"How do you know?"

"I *know*."

"I know" was her final answer to my probing.

Mom *always* had an explanation. Even if it didn't make sense to others, it made sense to her. She saw life through rose-colored glasses, and her advice, when requested, was always kind and encouraging. She found the good in every person and every situation. So *where was this indignation coming from?* I wondered. *And why couldn't she explain herself?* Sadly, I knew she would not be forthcoming with any sensible details, so I ended the conversation.

We drove in silence again for a couple of miles in heavy traffic.

"The ferry must be in," I said as we crept along.

No reply.

The last mile turned into ten long minutes, until finally we were next in line to go through the set of lights leading us to the highway that would take us home. I couldn't fight the urge to try to find the magic words that would snap her back to her senses.

"Mom, you don't know," I said quietly while looking into her bright-blue eyes.

"Peggy, no daughter in the world would *ever* not believe her mother," she screamed while pointing her accusatory finger at me. I shut down.

Over the next few weeks, she continued to plead her case about the people trying to kill everyone. We each did our best to agree to disagree.

~

Summer gave way to fall, and Mom made her way back to Florida, where cynical thoughts calmed down, thanks to a change of scenery and an easy living routine. Walking and basking in the beautiful southern air did prove to be very good for her. She kept busy through working, social-izing, and laughing—and life seemed to be getting better for a while. A number of years passed before the 9/11 stories diminished completely; however, new cryptic and confusing stories were on hand to take their place.

After a few years of commuting back and forth from Florida in a car, Mom decided it was getting to be a little too taxing. It was time to over-come her fear of flying. For the next few years, she flew back and forth while her car was transported by a professional business. In the spring of 2005, she altered the plan.

"Jocelyn told me about this transportation company that's half the price of what I've been paying," Mom told me over the phone.

"Wow, that sounds wonderful. Why don't you do it?" I replied.

"The problem is someone has to drive it half the distance. I'd rather have it go on a truck all the way." She didn't trust anyone to valet park her car. The thought of someone driving it halfway up the East Coast was troublesome.

"I think it'll be fine. Driving on the southern leg of the trip is easier on the car than the northern leg."

"The driver will take it to South Carolina. Then he'll put it on a transportation truck."

"What do you think you'll do?"

"It's a seven-hundred-dollar savings, so I think I'll do it."

Six long days after her return home, she anxiously stood out in the yard and thanked the man for his services as he pulled her little yellow Mustang back into the driveway. Not wanting to seem rude, she politely took her keys back from the man and waited until he was back in his massive vehicle and on his way before inspecting her own car scrupulously. She made two trips around her car as she inspected every inch before she opened the doors to gaze inside. She took pause at the driver's door, bending down to look closer, brushing at the door handle with a perturbed expression on her face. "What's this?" she asked.

She began complaining about some scratches on the driver's door and had a look on her face like she was smelling something really awful. But the situation seemed quite harmless—until the next morning.

"Peggy! Tom! Come look at this," she yelled from outside.

"What is it, Mom?" I asked. Mom took very good care of everything she owned and everyone she loved. She would be furious if anyone else treated her things any other way.

"Look! Right there! I told you there were scratches! You can see the scratches from where someone tried to break in!"

"Break in? That's a big leap from just some scratches."

"It's true."

"What do you mean, Mom? You think someone broke into your car?"

"Oh, I *know* someone tried to break in—look—just look!" she said, visibly upset.

Tom and I gave each other an uneasy glance. We didn't see any signs of foul play and were both really confused by her reaction.

"Let me take a look, Francesca," Tom said confidently, hoping to calm her back to her senses.

He knelt down close to the car and inspected the door around the handle and up around all the edges of the window. While his back was to her, he shot me a troubled look. Neither one of us saw any scratches at all, but Mom was convinced.

"Maybe there are a few minor scratches," Tom said, trying to appease her.

"See?" she retorted.

"I'll buff them out tomorrow, Francesca."

The following morning, Mom came down to breakfast with a blank stare.

"What's the matter, Mom?" I asked.

"I'm upset about those gouges in my car," she replied, "and the bloodstain in the back seat."

"A bloodstain?" You could have knocked me over with a feather.

She insisted I come out with her to investigate her accusation. "Yes, look, right there on the floor in the back seat. It's clear as day!"

"I don't see any bloodstains or any signs that a stain of any kind had been there, cleaned, or removed."

"Peggy, it's right there. In the back. On the floor."

"Mom, I don't see a stain at all."

"What do you mean you don't see it? It's right there!"

"I just don't see it, Mom. Whatever it is you think you see, I'm sure there's an explanation for it, but I don't think it's blood!"

"It's blood all right, and of course there's an explanation for it," she said and let it go for the day.

The next morning came with the explanation. Mom launched into a story that had all the makings of an Italian Mafia film. She knew it was all true.

"The man who transported my car back up north was in the mob. Somewhere along the way, he picked someone up, killed them, and then put him in the back seat, where the guy bled all over the place. Then he dropped the body off. I'm not exactly sure where, but I think somewhere in New Jersey. Then he put the car on the transportation truck," she said quite confidently, modifying the original transportation plan.

Tom and I stared at each other in disbelief, hearts sinking, stomachs churning. *Is she just joking?* I wondered.

The three of us stood in silence.

After several long seconds of her staring back at us in pure consternation, we knew she was serious. She gave me that look that reduced me to a scolded seven-year-old. That look that showed me how she maintained her dignity through years of abuse from her husband. That look that screamed, "I'm quirky—honor that!" That made me want to say, "You go, girl," while running away from her wrath. That alarmed me when I was young and made me proud as an adult. And it was that look in that moment I realized my mother's intrinsic fears had just then taken a very bizarre turn.

The story went on for weeks, taking a little different twist or turn, adding a new little detail here and there. Each time, I remained just as confused as before.

How does she know this? What is this all about? I wondered.

But life calls, children need tending to, work needs to get done, illogical stories blow over, and before you know it, order is restored—for a while, at least. My mother was seventy-one when she believed there was a murder in her Mustang.

~

The following two years involved confusing but harmless stories about friends and neighbors. Mom gave reports of people saying horrible things about her but couldn't repeat what they had said. The gossip upset her so much that she would refuse to socialize with the accused person, and the fact that she couldn't tell me what was said frustrated me. She began spending more and more time alone in her homes, north and south. One day while in her northern home, she declared she would not be attending a party for my grandson because our friend Sandra would be there.

"Why?" I asked.

"You would not believe what Sandra said to me," she replied.

I was really taken aback. Sandra is one of the kindest, sweetest people I know. I have never heard her say a bad word about anyone, anything, or any situation. It just wasn't her nature. "What did she say to you?" I asked.

"Never mind that."

Her response didn't make any sense. I pushed her a little more, hoping I could find a reasonable explanation for Sandra's comment and simply smooth things over. "What did she say, Mom?"

"It's too awful to repeat," she said and refused to discuss it any further.

Mom and I were always very candid with each other. We shared all our secrets, every deep, dark one of them. So for her to be holding back on me now just didn't make any sense. Still, over the course of three days she would not, or could not, bring herself to tell me what sweet Sandra said to her. At that, I went from perplexed to frustrated and finally dismissed her. She brought it up again the next day. "Peggy, why would Sandra say those awful things to me?"

"Mom, what did she say?" I asked firmly.

She made her bad-smell face and shook her head.

"Why won't you just tell me what she said?" I persisted. It was as if we were playing a game—your turn.

"Why won't you just believe me?" she snapped back.

"Mom, this is ridiculous. If you won't tell me what she said, I'm going to forget the whole thing."

She just stared at me.

"Fine. Stay home if you want." I didn't want to play anymore.

The next morning, I was fully prepared to go to the party without her when she walked into my room. "What time are we leaving?" she asked.

"Are you coming?" I said.

Am I crazy? I thought—*or was this just a new twist to the game?*

"Yes, of course," she said.

"Oh, good! We're leaving at two."

"OK, I'll be ready."

Seriously bizarre, I thought. I searched my mind to recollect the previous day's conversation. Did I misinterpret her concerns? Did I overreact? Or were we really playing a game?

But she was coming to the party, she was unfazed and happy, so I went back to what I was doing. Her nonchalant attitude carried on throughout the party, and she interacted with Sandra as if they were great friends. I watched in confusion and amazement.

~

When she returned to Florida, she had a new neighbor next door to her. Veronica, who was in her thirties, came from a wealthy Palm Beach family and couldn't manage to hold down a job. Instead she got involved with a "bad boy" who became her lover and got her hooked on drugs until Daddy sent her to rehab and then relocated her far away to the condo right next to my mother, in hopes that the boyfriend wouldn't find her. He did.

"They are doing drugs next door," she told me during our daily phone conversation.

"Mom, lots of people do drugs."

"Heroin?"

"How do you know they are doing heroin?"

Who shoots up in front of their neighbors? I thought.

"Because people come here all hours of the night to buy it," she said.

"How do you know *that*?"

"The police know that. And the drug dealers bang on my door all night long."

"Bang on your door?" Shivers went down my spine.

"They want to scare me so I won't say anything."

I was silent as I processed this development in my mother's new life of drama. *If this is true, it's not funny. If it isn't true, it's not funny,* I thought.

Veronica's drug use became the topic of our nightly conversation during the fall months. While the stories were cause for concern, I doubted they were true.

"He drives in the parking lot the wrong way so he can flash his lights in my window." That I believed. Everybody that entered the one-way parking lot through the exit flashed their lights in her window. I'm sure he knew better but was too lazy or arrogant or entitled to follow the rules.

"He moved the concrete parking block with my number on it to confuse me." That I did not believe. Those things are too heavy to move without a machine.

"He ran out of the condo and slammed the door while yelling obscenities." That I believed.

"He slammed the door so hard things fell off the wall." That I did not believe. I've been there when the wind slammed the door shut so hard the walls shook. Nothing ever fell off the wall.

"Mom, how does this behavior go on without any repercussions?" I asked.

"That's a damn good question," she replied.

"Why would the other people in the condo allow that?"

"They don't care."

I knew that wasn't a true statement. I would definitely look into it when I visited her in January.

~

While I was there for two weeks in January, I didn't witness any of the behavior she was referring to. I did see Veronica. She seemed quiet and kept to herself. Mom pointed out her boyfriend, but he didn't do anything out of the ordinary while I was there. Launching my own investigation, I learned from neighbors that she was in fact addicted to drugs, but no one knew of any late-night visitors, banging on doors, calling of police, or harassment by the boyfriend. Between the neighbors' accounts and Mom insisting her story was the truth, the whole truth, and nothing but the truth, I was left with two completely different sets of circumstances for each and every daily event.

When I left to go back up north, I had more questions than I'd had when I arrived—and was just as uneasy. As I sat in the southern airport feeling like an overcooked bowl of pasta, I began to cry.

A kind young woman sitting across from me responded to my tears. "Are you OK?" she asked.

"I'm leaving my mother here alone, and I'm really worried about her," I said through the lump in my throat.

"I know exactly how you feel. I'm doing the same thing."

"*Really*? Your mom's here, and you live in Boston?"

"Yes. You'd be surprised how common it is. It's so hard. But we can't force them to leave their homes just because it would be easier for us."

I immediately felt like I was welcomed into a secret club, which was oddly comforting. We talked for twenty minutes, mirroring each other's feelings and finishing each other's sentences like we'd known each other forever, until we parted ways. That chance encounter with a kind stranger sent from heaven would bring me comfort for years to come.

⌒

Mom and I spoke at least an hour each day. My intention was to use that hour thoughtfully and skillfully to somehow "fix" her. I thought if I forced her to fill in missing details, I could guide her back to reality. I was sure that once she got the Veronica story straight, other stories would fall into place. She would learn how to discriminate between true, false, embellished, and overlooked details. I was sure it would only take a few weeks—then boom—she would somersault across her gym mat, jump up on her own two feet, raise her hands high in the air, and be her old self again.

Alas, that never happened. Not only did I not make any progress, I regressed and retreated as I watched the situation intensify.

"Veronica overdosed at the twenty-four-hour store down the street," she stammered.

"Oh my goodness, what happened?" I asked.

"I don't know. There was blood everywhere. I think she went to the hospital, but she's home now."

"When did it happen?"

"In the middle of the night."

"How do you know what really happened? Did someone tell you?"

I was hoping that she had actually had a normal conversation with her neighbors and found out some factual information.

"No, I could hear them," she said, squashing my hopes.

"At the store?" I asked, knowing full well she wasn't in hearing distance.

"Yes, and I could see the police."

"At the store?" I asked, also knowing full well she couldn't see the store from her condo.

My mother could sleep through anything. The alarm clock would go off until it woke the neighborhood, and she still slept through it. I recollected a story about a time Uncle Fred spent the weekend with her in Florida. He extended his stay until Monday, when Mom's alarm went off to wake her for work.

"Jesus, Francesca. I thought you were dead!" Uncle Fred said to her.

"Oh? Why?" she asked.

"Didn't you hear the alarm? It's been going off for ten minutes."

She couldn't stop laughing long enough to give him a proper answer.

Even if the overdose commotion did somehow manage to wake her up, there was no way she could hear or see what was going on at the twenty-four-hour store down the street unless she left her home to investigate, and I knew that wouldn't happen. I wondered why my questions frustrated her, and I wondered why she couldn't answer them. I found myself doubting everything she said. Nothing made sense anymore. *That's enough*, I thought. *It's time to take the bull by the horns. I must get to the bottom of my mother's problem.*

FIVE

———— ～ ————

If you don't go out with your husband, someone else will.

—FRANCESCA JEAN

IT WAS A perfect July day that summer in 2009 when we invited our two friends Jack and Diane for an impromptu boat ride. With the cooler and picnic basket filled with dinner and drinks, we set out for an afternoon cruise to a local restaurant about thirty minutes away by boat—five minutes by car. As someone who is afraid of boats, water, and getting lost at sea, Mom decided to drive her car and meet us there.

The restaurant is located on a large marina and has an outside area for people to sit and relax while they wait to be called in to eat. We docked the boat, found a table, settled in, and kept a watchful eye out for Mom. Tom and Jack went to get drinks, while Diane and I sat and chatted. Mom joined us a few minutes later. Crowds of people were coming and going, wooden Adirondack chairs and benches were getting moved around constantly, and friends stopped by our table to chat.

"I think we should get going soon," I said after a couple of hours.

"I'm not done with my wine," Mom said.

"Well, you'll be all right here alone, won't you? I don't want to stay much longer."

"OK, Francesca, what seat would you like to keep? People will be coming by to steal away the others," Tom said.

She had been sitting on a wooden bench for two with a built-in table in the middle and a heart cut out at the top.

"I'll keep this one. You never know, someone may join me," she replied.

"Sounds like a plan, Francesca," Tom joked.

"I keep telling you to fix me up with a rich old man."

We all laughed at her unwavering good humor, and off we went.

When we returned home, Mom was in the kitchen waiting. "No one showed up," she said in an angry voice.

I just looked at her, confused.

"Tom said he was going to fix me up with someone."

"No, he didn't, Mom." I searched my mind to try to figure out where that thought came from.

"Then why did you tell me to keep the sweetheart bench?" she asked.

OK, I thought. *That makes sense. It's a leap, but a reasonable leap nonetheless. I can sort this out with her.*

"We didn't suggest the bench. We asked which one you wanted to keep," I said.

"Yes, you did," she quickly replied as if she had rehearsed her response.

"No, that was your choice. Tom asked what seat you wanted to keep, and you chose the bench."

"No, you guys told me to sit there because it was a sweetheart bench."

She had her thoughts in order and wasn't letting go. "Mom, you said, 'Oh, I may as well keep this one. You never know, someone might join me.'"

She shook her head as if she were erasing my words off a blackboard, wiping it clean for me to rewrite the correct answer.

"Mom, I'm sorry if you thought that, but no one had any plans of fixing you up with anyone."

She let it go for the rest of the day, but every day thereafter, she would revisit the events of that delightful afternoon in an attempt to get us to confess that our intentions all along were to have a man pounce on her after we left, and for some reason he simply didn't show up. Disappointed with the results, she scratched the restaurant fix-up and transitioned into a general fix-up.

I was in the kitchen making meatballs when Mom flew down the stairs to address me. "Who's coming to visit?" she asked at random and completely out of the blue.

"What do you mean?" I was in a constant state of confusion, as there were no indications of any events happening. "What? You mean the meatballs? They're for us."

"I don't like surprises," she continued.

"Mom, no one is coming."

"Should I get dressed up nice for this evening?"

"Where is this coming from?" I asked.

"Aren't you trying to fix me up with someone?"

"Mom, I swear to you. I *swear*—I am not fixing you up with anyone. I don't even believe in fixing people up. It's too complicated. I swear on the Bible—I am not, have no intentions of, and will not ever fix you up with anyone."

"Tom is," she said instantaneously.

I closed my eyes and took a deep breath.

"No, Mom, he's not. The same Bible swearing goes for him. Nobody that I know has any intentions of fixing you up." I was as sluggish with my remarks as she was as quick with hers.

"I heard you guys talking about it."

I tried to think of conversations I had had that would even remotely give her that impression; I really tried. And after a few quiet moments, I addressed her directly. "Listen, Mom, I don't know what you heard. But I give you my word, right here and right now, that neither Tom nor I, or anyone else we know, for that matter, is trying to fix you up with a man. Can we please just drop this fixing-up story? Please?"

"Well, why not? That might be nice," she retorted back as quick as a jackrabbit, spinning my head around like a top.

What? I thought. Not for a second did I think she *wanted* to be fixed up. I simply didn't understand her. One minute I was absorbed in how much cheese to add to the meatballs; the next I was processing some outlandish conversation about a man who had no name. For months I found myself constantly searching for ways to make sense of her bizarre thoughts and actions, her likes and dislikes, her quirks and her needs. Since living together as adults, we had had slight disagreements, but I went to great lengths to make her feel wanted and welcomed in my home…her home. I couldn't understand why she was being so difficult. Our perfectly-orchestrated dance had ended, and neither one of us knew how to deal with it. "*No. There will be no fix-ups. Ever. It's over. Please,*" I said forcefully.

But the thought was in her head, and all my attempts to alter that thought would fall on deaf ears. I stood helplessly as I watched the story develop and spin out of control until September came and she turned her focus to the journey back to Florida.

~

She returned to Florida safely, and we resumed our daily routine of hour-long phone conversations. The first couple of days were typical, with stories of settling in, old friends, walks, new restaurants, and warm weather. Later that week, she introduced a man into our daily conversations. A man with a girlfriend.

"There's a guy here who wants to date me, but he has a jealous girl-friend," she announced.

"Who?" I asked.

"Why won't she just let him go?"

"I don't understand. What man?"

"I don't know," she said indignantly. "You know him. Why won't you tell me his name?"

"What are you talking about?"

"He's the guy you and Tom tried to fix me up with."

"Mom, I told you a hundred times, we never tried to fix you up with anyone."

"Then who is this guy?"

"I don't know. You tell me."

"Tell you what? How can I tell you his name if I don't know him? You're telling me about this guy—so *you* tell *me* about him."

Abbot and Costello's "Who's on First" made more sense than our conversations.

"Never mind," she said.

I changed the subject.

Over the next two weeks, the story developed, and the man was now in love with her. With each phone call, I probed for details, trying to find some logic in her story, yet after each good-bye, I was left with more questions. I made myself a cup of herbal tea, went out on the deck, and called her.

"What's going on, Mom?" I asked.

"This girl is driving me crazy," she replied.

"What girl?"

"Oh, she's jealous of me. She wants to scratch my beautiful blue eyes out. That's what she said."

"Mom, who is this guy? What's his name? Who is this girl?" I was perplexed as to why she couldn't answer those simple questions—or just one. I would have settled for one. It was amazing how practiced she became at avoiding answering a question while still maintaining the conversation. She was the one driving the train, and that, my friends, was that!

"We've known each other for years. He wants to be with me, but this girl refuses to let him go."

"How come I've never heard about this man before?"

"You have. Wasn't I married to him at one point?"

There was a long pause in the conversation while my mind tried to wrap itself around *that* statement.

"Oh, I'm just kidding," she quipped with a giggle.

Our daily conversations were becoming quite obscure. Weeks passed, and I still hadn't been able to get any real answers about the man and his girlfriend. I poured myself a glass of wine and went out on the deck to call her. "How's it going, Mom?" I asked.

"This bitch is out to get me," she replied.

"Who?"

"Killa!" Mom finally gave the girlfriend a name. Killer—pronounced Killa by New England standards.

"Who's Killa?"

"She's the girlfriend. She's trying to kill me."

"How do you know these things?" I asked constantly.

"I heard them talking. They were paddleboarding together, and I heard them fighting about me."

What? I thought. "Where were they paddleboarding? Was it close enough so that you could hear them talking?"

"In the marina. I could hear them from here."

Logistically there is no way that could happen. I was stunned and quiet.

"Peggy, it's true. She wants to kill me."

"Mom—"

"She doesn't want to share him with me, so she's out to get me."

"How do you know all this?"

"Oh, I know, all right."

"Start at the beginning. What is this guy's name?"

"What are you talking about? You know him!" she barked in anger.

I felt my request for more information was perfectly justified. She viewed my request as challenging her truth. Like a bear protecting her cubs, she became indignant. I changed the subject.

The phone calls went on and on while she remained true to her story without any evidence or explanation. Night after night, she managed to dance around my questions without giving me any answers. We were both frustrated and angry. She was convinced I had the ability to fill in the blanks of her stories and was angry at me for not granting her wishes.

I was frustrated that she wouldn't fill in her own blanks or admit that she could not. Neither one of us was capable of satisfying the other. Our daily phone call ritual was becoming more of a chore and less of a choice. I took my drink out to the deck and called her.

"What are we going to do about Killa?" she asked.

I was astonished by her urgency. She knew by the caller ID that it was me, so she skipped the hello and went right to her nonsensible saga.

With each passing day, Killer grew increasingly wicked, and her sole desire in life was to kill my dear, sweet mother. I continued with the daily phone calls, trying to make sense of the man who was in love with her but had a jealous girlfriend. For hours and hours, days and days, weeks and weeks, and months and months, I pined over how something so real to her could made no sense at all to me. I asked her questions until she abruptly ended the conversation in frustration. She may not have had any answers to my questions, but she knew what she knew. It was a standoff, and we were about to shoot it out for the win.

I took a deep breath and dialed her number.

"I've been banned from the RiverView," Mom announced, skipping *hello* again.

"Excuse me, *what*?" I gulped.

While spending time with my mother in Florida, the RiverView is my favorite place to go out to eat. It's a laid-back restaurant that sits on the Intracoastal Waterway. People not only drive to it but also dock their boats, jump off, and grab a bite to eat. Similar to the northern restaurant with the sweetheart bench and Adirondack chairs, it has delicious food, a great happy hour, sun, birds, fresh air, beautiful sunsets, two tiki bars, and familiar faces. If I didn't go out to eat anywhere else while visiting Florida, it would be just fine with me.

"What do you mean you've been banned from the RiverView?" I asked.

"There were two women sitting at the bar right across from me, and they must have seen me because they started fighting over him."

I was silent while I listened to her story with my stomach all twisted in knots. "But who were you with?"

"I was all alone, minding my own business. He must have been there or was coming there. The women saw me and starting fighting."

"So why are you banned from the place?"

"I guess because he loves me. They're all in it together."

I was completely dumbfounded, and my eyes grew moist as a wave of profound sadness overcame me. My sweet, sweet mother would *never* be involved in *any* action or altercation that would result in management banning her from *anywhere*! It's just that simple. My father? Yes. My mother? Never!

"But, Mom," I said, determined to get to the bottom of this, "did you get in the middle of the fight? They can't just say 'You over there minding your own business, you're out of here!'"

"Well, they did."

Grudgingly, I pushed for details, but I knew I wouldn't get any that made sense. And more importantly, deep down, I knew it wasn't true. "You can't be banned," I said.

"Well, that's what they said. I'm telling you, she won't be happy until I'm dead."

"Who were the two ladies?"

"Friends of hers."

The more I probed for details from her, the more she looked to me to fill in the blanks. It was exasperating.

～

Over the following months, more illogical stories began to develop. Tales that rolled slow and steady, like waves on the ocean, building and building until they crashed—incoherently and without basis—on the shore. They started with teasers to catch my interest, in hopes that I would believe her. When I didn't jump right in with the vigor of a sixteen-year-old gossip queen, she tried to make them more convincing by adding details to prove her point and back up her story. The painful conversations went on forever, consuming her thoughts, actions, and well-being. Umpteen times after ending a conversation with her, I thought about calling her to tell her about the conversation I'd had with this irrational woman! That's what I did when I had a story to share or a problem to solve. I called my mother.

Suddenly, that gift was gone.

Realizing that what she was going through had begun to affect her daily living, I started sharing my story and searching for answers elsewhere. It was painfully obvious that she wasn't able to provide them, at least not during our phone calls. I was consumed with worry about her. She started to feel panicked when she had to go to the local grocery store—something she did almost daily. She was convinced that a woman who worked at the store was giving her dirty looks. My curiosity as to why this woman would behave like that toward my sweet mother raised the curtain to a whole new saga. This time, the teasers had to do with my father—and when it came to my father, anything was possible or plausible.

My parents were divorced. My father lived on the west coast of Florida, and she resided on the east coast. He really didn't have a relationship with my mother or his children other than a yearly visit for a couple of hours. But I took the bait.

"Your father went out with her, so she doesn't like me," she insisted.

"How do you know Dad went out with her?" I replied.

"I know!"

Of course she just knew; how silly of me to ask. The story about the woman in the store with the dirty looks went on for a few weeks. My mother came up with a new scenario every day. As it all seemed relatively harmless, I listened while she shared her thoughts—until the woman became aggressive.

"She pushed a grocery cart right at me," she said during our phone chat.

"Did you tell anyone?" I asked.

"Peggy!" she yelled, as if to snap me out of my stupidity. "She was talking about me to the woman at the next cash register loud enough for everyone to hear." She wanted me to believe that everyone in the store knew about the bad behavior, yet no one did anything about it. I wasn't doing anything about it either, and that frustrated her.

"Mom, that can't be true. Are you sure?"

"Yes, I'm sure. And yesterday she interrupted a conversation I was having with my friend."

"What friend?"

"Peggy, they all know!"

Why can't you, just once, just tell me the name of the friend? I thought. *Why can't she answer the simple questions?* At least then I could confirm her story. "Who was with you?"

"Never mind. I have to go."

I thought about my options. I could keep digging. I could also just stop calling Mom and detach myself from the stories. My heart grew heavy with the thought of isolating her by ending our daily phone calls and altering our relationship, but I wasn't sure how much more of the guessing game I could handle. I dialed her number. Maybe this one would be the phone call that made sense.

"Do you have any plans for your birthday, Mom?" I tried to stay away from the story of the lady in the grocery store.

"No, I'm not going anywhere," she replied.

"How's Jocelyn doing? Is she in Florida?"

"No, she's up north. Peggy, what are you going to do about this woman?"

"What woman?" I asked, knowing full well who she was talking about.

"The woman in the grocery store who hates me."

"Mom, why would she hate you?"

"Because of Dad. She's jealous."

"How do you know she went out with Dad? Did you talk with the woman? Did you talk with Dad?"

"I know. He went out with her, took money from her, then he broke off the relationship by telling her he was still in love with me."

My father did work at the same chain of grocery stores. He did sleep with other women while married to her. I believe he remained in love with her. He did take money from people, and he kept very few, if any, commitments. So, it *was* a plausible story—but not a very *probable* one.

When it became obvious I wasn't going to get a definitive answer, I gave up and changed the subject. But the troubling fact remained that for my mom, going to the store had become uncomfortable and frightening. If the woman wasn't working that day to upset her, Killer was there to harm her. My fear that something was terribly wrong was becoming inescapable.

The Killer stories continued daily, and eventually, Killer formed her very own "posse." The posse lived in an old hotel just a block away, making it convenient for them to look in my mother's windows at night, chase her with guns blasting while she went out for a walk, pound on her door in the middle of the night, and try to break the lock while she was at work. She called the police to show them where the lock was tampered with, but alas, they could not see what she reported. She saw Killer at her work a number of times. One evening she told me her boss was upset about Killer showing up at the club.

"I quit work today," she said.

"Why, Mom?"

"The club members don't like Killa coming around."

I called her friend and colleague Mary to confirm her story. She had no idea who Killer was. "No, Peggy, she said she was retiring. It was her idea, not ours," said Mary.

Killer and her posse went everywhere my mother went. She began to spend all her free time in the home, going out only when it was absolutely necessary. She was in full-blown distress and couldn't understand why the police didn't do anything to help her, so she assumed Killer was in "cahoots" with law enforcement. Mom used that term often, as if everyone was in cahoots with everyone else as part of the world's main objective to destroy her. She told me about the neighborhood meetings and the neighbors who were in cahoots with Killer.

"They're all in on it," she said during our phone conversation.

"What do you mean?" I asked.

"I saw everyone coming out of Annie's condo last night. They were having a meeting with Killer."

I envisioned Annie bringing a few neighbors in to show off a new piece of furniture or share a new magazine she just finished reading.

"Annie?" I asked, sick to my stomach.

Annie is a widow with two grown children. She had lived next door to my mother for twenty years. She is also a devout Catholic who is kind, sweet, and honest. My mother watched her children grow up and loved every minute of their accomplishments as well as their shenanigans. Annie, who wouldn't harm a flea, also practiced at the same church my mother attended. And now sweet Annie was the star of yet another one of Mom's stories.

As any good parishioner would tell you, it's not uncommon for people to attend the same Mass, sit in the same pew, and congregate toward the same group of attendees. For my mother, it was Sunday's ten o'clock Mass, and she always sat toward the front of the church, next to a handsome, single man. That was fine for a while. He liked her, she liked him, and nothing happened beyond the church walls—until three ladies got very upset and formed a plot to get her thrown out of church.

"Seriously? Three jealous ladies?" I asked. I pictured three women holding hands during the "Our Father" and lifting them up to God as they persecuted my mother under their breath.

"Yes, they told me I couldn't come to their church anymore," she replied.

"Who told you that?" I asked in anger.

"The three ladies. They wrote a letter to the bishop."

"What letter? Did you see a letter?"

"I saw it."

"Where did you see it?"

"Annie had it."

"What does it say? Read it to me." *Aha, finally something concrete,* I thought—for less than a second.

"I don't have it anymore, but I read it and I know what it says."

"That doesn't make any sense. You wouldn't get rid of a letter like that. I know you too well." I flashed back to a time when I was about ten. I had found a piece of paper on the side of the road with my mother's name handwritten on it and brought it to her. It was page one of a multi-page letter that a neighbor wrote and then threw in the trash. My mother made me go back to that trash can to dig through garbage until I came back with every page. She held on to it for a year.

"Peggy, I saw the letter. It was from the bishop, and it said I could not attend that church anymore. I had the letter, and then I didn't have it. I don't know where it is, but I know there was a letter, and I know those three ladies had something to do with his decision."

Wow, I thought. *This is preposterous. What is going on with her?*

I thought about all the stories she told me: banned from a restaurant, bullied out of the grocery store, expelled from the neighborhood church, consumed with fear that people wanted to kill her—and all within a couple of months! I couldn't wrap my brain around what was going on in my mother's world, but I absolutely didn't believe that last story. I had been a lifelong practicing Catholic, and I worked at a Catholic church for fifteen years. The one thing I knew for sure was that there wasn't a Catholic bishop in this country who would ban someone from entering the building for sitting in the wrong pew! For months, I thought if I could reason with her and help her with details one story at a time, her brain would remember how to methodize consecutive thought processes. Having exhausted that plan with catastrophic results, I was running out of ideas. At the end of my rope and without adequate rationale, I tried tough love.

"Nope, Ma, I don't believe it. I don't believe you."

"Well, it's true," she said softly, as if beaten down with sadness.

So much for that tactic. She didn't snap out of it—and I felt like an uncaring bully.

SIX

That's not normal.

—Francesca Jean

THE PAINFUL PHONE conversations continued throughout the fall and into the winter. I was working with children in the religious education department and was fortunate to have two weeks off in the winter. I took them around school vacation, so I could extend the visit to almost three weeks. Tom would be away at sea for six weeks, John and Daniel were all grown up and on their own, and Matthew was in college. My wonderful boss had a philosophy that family was of the utmost importance, and as long as I had things covered at work, it was decreed that I should go spend time with my mother. I had always made a point to spend at least a week or two every year with my mother in Florida. I believe it's important to develop relationships with the people your loved ones spend so much time with, so I was thrilled to manage a three-week period, in hopes of getting to the bottom of what was going on with her.

While on my 2010 visit to Florida, I tried many approaches to talk with my mother about Killer and the two-timing boyfriend. I wanted to understand, because I still wanted to believe her. I was hoping to make sense of the stories. I hoped they had a true baseline that went anywhere from somewhat enhanced to extremely embellished. Maybe she was overwhelmed and needed some help with understanding and clarification. I tried taking her out to dinner so that I would have her undivided attention, devoid of any distractions a home may bring—like mirrors to look into with every pass, drawers to clean, tables to clear, or news to watch. I tried having her write down details as she remembered them by putting a pad of paper on the island in the kitchen and asking her to write things down as they popped into her head, but the paper remained blank. I tried asking her to explain the various stories slowly, piece by piece. I stopped her for reality checks, asked questions, and did my best to break down thoughts and sequences. But she simply couldn't fill in the missing details. She was absolutely sure the details were true, but she could never get beyond her hypothesis. Inevitably, she would get angry with me and dismiss me as a heartless, uncaring daughter.

"But Mom, what about—?" I pushed.

"Never mind," became her safety words.

I dropped the conversation only to revisit it later with a lump in my throat, tears behind my eyes, and a profound sadness as I knew she would not be able to make any sense out of the stories.

~

When I returned home, the process continued with our phone calls. Sometimes I would try a new tactic, but typically I responded with a knee-jerk reaction. The process became utterly predictable: I dug for details. She became frustrated. I kept challenging her. She became angry. I became angry. Neither one of us was ever satisfied with the ending. On one occasion she was so upset with me she hung up on me and refused to answer my return call. She'd never done that before, so I was afraid she'd added me to her list of severed relationships. I called my brother and asked him to call her to see if she was OK. "She won't answer my call," I told him.

"OK. I'll try and see what's up," he replied.

He called me back to tell me she was fine and she that made no mention of our discussion. She only shared her confused thoughts with her daughter. Her behavior was our dirty little secret, and she would vehemently deny loss of control to anyone other than me.

Mom decided that her only option was to remain safely in her home, so she proceeded to shut herself in most of the day and positively the entire night. When I visited her in Florida, I was no longer allowed to chat with neighbors or sit outside after seven o'clock each evening, something I adored doing while escaping the harsh New England weather. When the sun went down, the doors were bolted shut until morning. I wasn't allowed to sleep with my windows open and had to keep my blinds closed most of the time. Listening to her yell at me, watching her fear, and feeling her heart break because of my betrayal was too difficult for me. I only pushed so far before giving in.

With all the alone time, her thoughts began to paralyze her. Her friends began calling me, one by one.

"Peggy, something is seriously wrong with Francesca," her friend Jess informed me.

"What's going on?" I asked.

"She won't speak to me anymore. When I call, she answers and hangs up on me."

"What happened?"

"She got lost in the crowd at the boat parade. She didn't know where she was, and she's been acting really weird."

"I'm so sorry. I know something is going on with her. I just don't know what to do."

"Well, you need to do *something*. You don't want the police to Baker Act her."

"What do you mean? What's Baker Act?"

"In Florida, the police can take her to a mental institution for a three-day period to have her evaluated if they think she is in danger of harming herself or others."

"I don't think she'll do anything like that!"

"Something is wrong with her, Peggy, and she needs to be evaluated. But there are some scary institutions in the area, so it would be better if you do it. That way, you can choose the place."

How the hell am I going to pull that one off? I thought.

"OK, thanks Jess. I'll work on it," I said.

"Let me know if I can help."

~

Every police car that went down the street was there for Killer. Every fire truck, EMT team, and ambulance in the area was there for Killer. Every beat-up car that passed by had a member of Killer's posse driving it, with the sole purpose of keeping a watchful eye on my mother. They were building wooden boxes to bury her in after the deed was done. When Killer wasn't devouring Mom's rational thoughts, her posse took her place. She saw men hiding in bushes, bullets flying through the air that missed her head by inches, and chunks of the door to her condo hacked off by Killer's posse.

Mom was in a downward spiral—and she was taking me with her.

The following years were a roller coaster of calm and chaos, neither state a healthy one for either us. The calm manifested in the form of spending most of my time on the couch. The chaos involved fits of frustration and erratic crusades of advocacy. I imagined that a world with sisters would solve all my problems, as often as my mother imagined that winning the lottery would solve all of hers. *Sisters would understand. Sisters would care. Sisters would help.* I was angry at my siblings for being male and uninvolved. Although they each had their reasons— one brother was stationed in the Middle East, one brother had a young family and a child with autism, and one brother couldn't help—it was all too obvious to others.

"Are you an only child?" was a common reaction from strangers.

"What's up with your brothers?" friends asked constantly.

"I don't get it" were the compassionate words that accompanied the hugs I received from family.

"It is what it is," I replied.

I was angry at all the doctors my mother visited in Florida for not being able to come up with a diagnosis and angry at the Internet for lack of information. I was angry at my mother for not making any sense, for not allowing me to attend her doctor appointments, and for being so paranoid that it prevented me from enjoying my visits to Florida. I was angry and sad and depressed and anxious, but what hurt more deeply than all of the above was the fact that I was losing my best friend.

Mom was angry too, although she refused to reveal any negative thoughts in front of others. Even though her quality of life went from healthy, happy, and active to merely getting through the day, she always had a smile on her face. My quality of life changed along with hers because I let it. My smile only came out on special occasions. I had somewhat normal days when I could manage to get things done, followed by what I called "crash-and-burn" days with overloaded feelings of frustration and defeat that would render me incapacitated. I knew I needed help, but my sweet therapist had long since retired, so I reached out to find a replacement. Someone at work recommended I see Dr. Jones.

"She's very spiritual," my colleague said. I was blessed to work with a saint of a woman. She was like a second mother to me. She found God in every person she met—bar none.

"But is she any good?" I asked, knowing the answer would be influenced by her halo.

"People love her."

"I'll give her a try." I was too beaten down to fight.

Dr. Jones was in her midsixties and semiretired. She spent three months in New England (where she practiced) followed by a month down south (where she relaxed). Her plan was to phase out her work up north over the next few years and live full time in the South. Her office was large and tidy, and she was pleasant and kind. At our first meeting, Dr. Jones said all the right things, or at least all the right things I already knew.

When she repeated all the right things that I already knew at the second, third, fourth, and fifth meetings, I began to phase her out. I saw her seven times over a nine-month period and ended the relationship feeling just as frustrated as I did when I entered it. She acknowledged on our first meeting that in order for progress and healing, it's important the doctor/patient relationship clicks. We didn't click.

~

One day, I was chatting with my son John's friend Katy.

"How are you, Peggy?" she asked.

"Ugh," I replied. Tom said often, "Don't ask Peggy how she's doing, because she'll tell you," so the people who were close to my heart knew that a one-word answer spoke volumes.

"You should try Reiki."

Katy is one of those people who lights up the lives of everyone she touches. She is very dear to me, and I knew I should listen.

"Really?" I said. "I've been intrigued by Reiki for a while now."

"It helps me. My family thinks I'm crazy but I Reikied my grandmother the other day. She really didn't know what I was doing, but she said she felt better than she had in a very long time."

"Hmmm."

It was just the boost I needed to follow through on something that had already been on my mind, and the impetus for my fourth love affair with therapy.

Katy gave me the name of her Reiki master, so I called her and began on a journey that would not only change me profoundly but save me from deep despair and depression. Mary, my lifesaver, would become my therapist, my friend, my teacher, and my very special gift from God.

Mary is beautiful, kind, genuinely caring, and has a powerful presence. We connected immediately. "Have you ever had Reiki before?" she asked.

"No, but I've been thinking about it for a while," I said.

I thought I was going to experience the art of Reiki and nothing more, but she informed me that she was a therapist; a therapist who is also a Reiki master—or a Reiki master who is also a therapist. "However, first we talk."

And talk we did, for ninety minutes, followed by a thirty-minute Reiki session. She gave; I received. The experience far exceeded anything I had ever been through. Notwithstanding the amazing therapeutic aspect, the session was from a place of love and caring beyond my wildest dreams.

"How do you feel?" Mary asked.

"Amazing," I replied.

I left with a follow-up appointment and what I called homework. On the drive home, I could feel my body letting go of negative feelings and counterproductive thoughts about my mother. Ten minutes after I left her office, my sinuses started to drain, my stomach rumbled, and my mouth made a gesture like it was dry heaving, purging out negative thoughts and feelings. I could never have imagined how much Mary would become part of my life and my healing on this journey with my mother. She assured me that, although challenging, everything would be OK, and she was going to help me through this difficult life lesson.

Therapy gave me the strength to manage the heavy situation and to become organized enough to get through a week or so until the next crash and burn. To say I was "having a difficult time holding it together" would be an understatement, so I was seeing Mary three times a month. The sessions left me with a fresh, new outlook on life—or what she called a "new pair of shoes." The journey, she explained, was so difficult my metaphorical shoes would wear out in a matter of days.

Mom's behavior consumed the entire house and changed our way of life. Sadness, frustration, confusion, anxiety, and fear now filled our once-happy home. And Tom missed his partner. Our evening talks went from a variety of interesting topics to just one: my mother—night after night after night after night. I became obsessed with watching her and her behaviors, trying to find that one act or action that would lead me to a moment of clarity. Like a night watchman, she stared at the outside world from her safe place on the inside of the window. If she were to venture out, she'd have to gather her armor and, if available, a protector. When she was home up north, she was never alone.

"What are you looking at, Mom?" I asked as I watched her stare out the window.

"Oh, nothing. Are those kids supposed to be in the trees?" she inquired.

"I think they're OK." Sometimes my reply would be "What kids?" But today I didn't want the fight.

She took a long look and then just stopped moving—like she was hit with one of those time-stopping guns in the movies. I inadvertently mimicked her—both of us unaware that we were motionless for at least fifteen minutes, her staring out the window; me staring at her.

"What is she doing?" I asked Mary.

"Never mind what she's doing; what are *you* doing?" she questioned back.

~

Now back in Florida, Mom began dismissing the once-dear friends she had had for many years and made wonderful memories with.

"Why won't you speak to Jess?" I asked.

"Peggy, she was really mean to me. And I think she's friends with someone Killa knows," she said.

"I don't believe that's true."

"She grabbed my arm really hard at the boat parade and told me I was lost. I knew exactly where I was."

"That's not a reason to end a friendship."

"She yelled at me!"

"Just talk to her about it," I said.

"You'll see. You'll start weeding out your friends before too long."

I followed up with phone calls, one friend at a time, either apologizing for her because she didn't want to see them any longer or explaining to them that the wild stories of people trying to kill her were not true, asking them to divert the conversation onto something a bit more pleasant.

"You know, Peggy, I thought that story a little strange," her friend Maryanne said.

"I can't figure out what's going on with her," I said.

"I said to her, 'Oh Francesca, if they were really trying to kill you, you'd be dead by now!'"

"I know; she's making things up. I just don't know what is true and what is totally fabricated."

"She's pretty convincing, Peggy."

I had a very difficult time explaining to the people who didn't spend a lot of time with her that there was anything wrong with her at all. The only people who believed me were the people who lived in the same condominium building with her. They believed me because they witnessed her daily paranoid behavior. But my mother forbade me to speak with them, so it was difficult to collaborate with them to find answers. I couldn't bear to see the painful face of betrayal she exhibited the few times I did hobnob with a neighbor or two, so I could only manage to sneak in short conversations out of her view behind the dumpster while out on my morning walk.

I walked by Dina's window and motioned for her to meet me outside. Dina had purchased the condominium four doors down twelve years earlier when she left the apartment she rented across the street. She was a proud, lifelong single woman who made it her business to greet neighbors, their children, and their pets. If anyone had a question about someone who lived in the community, they stopped at Dina's door to get an answer.

"What do you know about this man that my mother keeps talking about?" I asked her.

"What's his name?" she asked.

"Harry Tambini." My mother had finally given the mystery man a name a few months earlier.

"I don't know anything about him."

"Really? My mother said you knew him. She said you were thrilled when he stopped seeing her and proposed to Killa."

"No, Peggy. I've never even heard that name before. Who's Killer?" she pronounced correctly.

"She said you came out of the laundry room saying, 'Tambini is free. Tambini!'"

"No," said Dina, shaking her head. "Maybe that's why she won't speak to me."

"What happened with that?"

"I don't know. I said hello to her in the laundry room, and she wouldn't answer me."

"I'm sorry. You guys were such good friends."

"A few weeks later, I asked if I did something to offend her, and she gave me an evil look and told me I knew exactly what I did."

"Something's really wrong, Dina."

"I know. I figured she was ill. A few of us have noticed. I just stay away from her and watch over her from afar. I don't want to upset her."

"Thanks, I really appreciate that."

"We all care about her very much. We all watch out for her. Who's Killer?" she asked again.

"No one," I answered with a sigh.

That's where I got confirmation that her two-timing boyfriend was nonexistent, as was his Killer girlfriend and her posse. That's where I learned that her paranoid behavior was rapidly increasing and the whole neighborhood witnessed it daily. That's where I learned for sure that something was very wrong and I needed to get her some help as soon as possible—out of her view, behind the dumpster.

Having her neighbors confirm that something really was wrong reinforced my urgency to find out what that something was. I loved her dearly, and I owed her that—even if I had to do it with her kicking and screaming. *She* knew something was wrong, but she couldn't deal with the prospects, so she chose to stay in her happy little denial bubble.

"If I get cancer, I don't want to know about it," she had told me throughout my life.

"How is that even possible, Mom?" I would respond.

"Make it possible."

"Seriously?"

"Really, Peggy, don't tell me! I don't want to know!"

Happy little bubble.

I went to work, secretly copying down the names of the pills she was taking. After researching side effects and talking with drug experts until I exhausted all possibilities, I gave up that theory. I wrote a letter to her doctor but never got a response. I wrote another letter nine months later and again heard nothing. I spent hours on the computer and spoke with anyone who would listen. After months of searching with no answers or input from anyone, for the time being I settled on elderly schizophrenia. I wasn't really sure—not sure at all, in fact, but I needed something to grasp on to, and that diagnosis explained her hallucinations.

As time went on, I was angry, lost, frustrated, helpless, and increasingly desperate. I didn't have any support from her primary care physician, and I didn't have sisters. My journaling was growing dark and angry, but I kept going back into past writings, hoping to find an answer. I was mad all the time. I was extremely frustrated that no one seemed to care enough to help me find a diagnosis. Against my own doctor's advice, I took her to my primary care physician that summer of 2010. I would have to pay out of pocket. The initial visit wasn't a great expense, but the office frowned upon out-of-pocket visits because follow-up treatment could be expensive without insurance coverage and referrals. But at that point, I didn't care. That's all there was to it: I was desperate! I needed help from someone in the medical profession, and if I had to get it myself and pay for it myself, so be it. My mother wasn't happy about it, but she eventually acquiesced.

Mom and my doctor went into the room together. He explained that he was going to ask her a series of questions and chat with her a bit and then call me into the room.

"There is nothing wrong with your mother," he declared.

"See?" said my mother as she sat up high on the table.

"She can count backwards. She has no trouble retrieving words. She is up on current events."

She can also stand on her head, I added without speaking.

"She's a perfectly delightful lady," he said.

I was really hoping that she wouldn't be able to put one over on you, I thought but desperately wanted to scream out loud.

"Did she tell you that people are trying to kill her?" I asked.

He jerked back in his chair. "Do you think people are trying to kill you?" he asked her.

"Oh, I *know* people are trying to kill me!" she said confidently.

Thank you, Jesus, I prayed quietly and sincerely.

"OK, I'm going to draw some blood, run some tests, and would like to see her again next week."

When we returned home, she jumped into her comfort zone and refused to go back. I spent the next two days reasoning, pleading, and begging—all in vain.

~

Mom mastered the art of concealing her symptoms in front of almost everyone. With the exception of the Killer stories that drove her closest friends and family members berserk, she was able to maintain an ordinary lifestyle. She had long since dismissed any thoughts of doing anything extraordinary. If she were to experience anything grand or amazing, it would have to come to her. She was happy to attend family parties, take long walks to the beach, go out to a late lunch or early dinner with Tom and me, or just sit out on our deck on a beautiful day and have a glass of wine. I relished those moments and was pleased to join her in that happy denial bubble.

Maybe it was just a quirky phase she was going through, I hoped in those normal moments.

But she couldn't maintain that façade. At the end of the day, I was her soft pillow to fall on.

And then reality came through the door like a hurricane.

When I shared my concerns with people, most looked at me with a blank stare, as if I were speaking a language they didn't understand. The behavior I witnessed on a daily basis was hard to grasp. They didn't see her when she let her guard down. They didn't see her tantrums when she sundowned. They didn't see her on her bad days. They saw her at parties, when she was in her finery, or at home for short visits, when she was at her best. And when she did shine, it was brightly! For the most part, Mom really was a pleasure to be around, and only a few chosen people were allowed to see her when she wasn't at her best. Yet I still couldn't fathom why more people in her life didn't see her failing. All I could do was keep trying.

My attempts to help people understand the vast difference in the behavior they witnessed from their beloved Francesca and the behavior I described about my mother was extremely confusing. People listened, stared, and moved on. But my cousin Audrey stared at me longer than most—and stayed.

She wanted an explanation. "I'm not getting it, Peg," she lamented.

"You know when you have the flu and it knocks you out to the point where you just can't get out of bed. But sometimes you have something really important to do, and so you have no choice—you just have to rally. It's like that," I said.

Audrey nodded, acknowledging she was following my thought process.

"You manage to get yourself up, showered, dressed, go to the doctor, or appointment, or accomplish whatever task needs attention—and then you come home and crash on the couch."

"Oh! I get it."

"That's what it's like."

"That's a good analogy, Peg."

"You see her at the appointment—I see her at home."

"Ahhh."

That in itself is a testament to my mother's strength as well as her denial. She was resilient, strong-willed, and a fighter, and managed to fool many—including professionals. It was truly hard to grasp the reality of the situation until you actually witnessed her behavior. True understanding only came with seeing.

One day, my friend joined my mother and me on our daily walk. It was a typical uneventful two-mile walk to the beach and back. When we got back to my home, Mom couldn't hold back; she needed to express her fear.

"Did you see that car almost hit me?" she asked.

"No, Mom, I didn't see any cars even come close to us," I said.

"Well it did! Someone was trying to run me over!"

"I didn't see it," I said softly.

It was a typical occurrence for me, but as I glanced over to make eye contact with my friend to claim quiet confirmation that my concern was justified, her deer-in-headlights expression granted me my request. She was stunned.

Later that day, Mom asked my son John if he knew Killer.

"What are you talking about, Nonni?" he replied in horror.

John was now living in his own home with his wife and their three children. He rarely had one-on-one time with his grandmother and was shocked by her question. It was one thing to hear the stories from his mother, half listening while chasing after children. It was quite another to have his grandmother engage him into them.

"Oh, I thought you knew her," Mom said as she left the room.

John watched her walk up the stairs and waited until he heard her footsteps above him.

"What the heck, Ma?" he asked.

"My dear child, what do you think I've been trying to tell you?" I asked.

While John managed to escape Mom's bizarre behavior on a daily basis, mild-mannered Matthew did not. He addressed his grandmother's hallucinations with thoughtful, kind responses. Like the time she wanted one of my floor lamps out of the house—immediately.

"Matthew, would you please take this lamp to the basement? It stinks," she said.

"What? Nonni, I can't smell anything," he said as he gave the lamp a sniff.

"Pffftt. Matthew—it stinks to high heaven."

Matthew looked over to me for approval. I put my arms out, palms up, giving him permission to appease his grandmother.

"OK, off to the basement you go," Matthew replied.

~

Toward the end of August, Mom's routine was to start thinking about returning to Florida, which meant spending a lot of time in her room preparing for the transition. Tom can pack for a trip—whether it be days, weeks, or months, abroad or domestic—in an hour or two. Mom packed for months. In the end, she fit everything in one small carry-on. Matthew takes after his Nonni; he spends an exorbitant amount of time packing. We call it the "travel dance." When Matthew does the travel dance, he drives us all crazy, but when Mom did the travel dance, we loved it. It kept her mind occupied and gave us a much-appreciated reprieve from the Killer stories. For her, it was good to have something else to focus on, something to look forward to. For us: quiet!

SEVEN

———— ～ ————

Watch out! You might slip on a banana.

—FRANCESCA JEAN

A WEEK INTO my February 2011 visit to Florida, Mom and I decided to catch up with a couple of friends for dinner and drinks. We all met at a restaurant at six o'clock, but the place was packed, so instead of waiting an hour for a table, we chose to sit at the bar and eat there. Mom and I shared a bottle of wine, an appetizer, and a burger. The four of us were chatting away, having a grand time, sharing food, swapping stories, and enjoying drinks. As it was getting toward the end of the night, I realized the bottle of wine was just about empty. I knew I hadn't had that much to drink, as I was driving.

Oh boy, I thought. That meant Mom drank way too much wine.

She was never a big drinker. One glass of wine would normally take her three hours to drink. She'd only have another on special occasions. Once in a while, she would have a sweet after dinner drink, but she would continually add ice to the liquor, making the drink last for hours. Other than those few occasions, I had never seen her drink hard liquor. She did sometimes ask someone for a sip of a martini or a drink that was intriguing, but the minute the glass touched her lips, she pulled back.

Alarm bells went off in my head, and sure enough, when we got up to leave the restaurant, she was pretty tipsy. I helped her to the car while she wobbled and giggled. When we got home, she took her time drinking water, brushing her teeth, and getting ready for bed. Brushing her teeth was a nightly ritual that took thirty minutes, and one she never missed. She would get out her yarn and floss every tooth meticulously.

"Francesca, you'll have the best-looking teeth in the graveyard!" Tom would tell her.

"I spent a lot of money on these teeth," she informed him every time.

She stayed up for over an hour, hydrating herself with water and walking off her fuzzy head before going to bed.

The next day, my cousin Bella picked us up and took us to lunch. We chose a table outside on the patio at a lovely restaurant overlooking the Intracoastal Waterway. Bella and I each ordered a glass of wine. My mother ordered sparkling water.

"Cheers," we said.

Moments later, Mom stood up.

"Where you going, Mom?" I asked.

"I don't know," she replied.

"Are you OK?"

"I don't know."

"Wait, I'll go with you," I said.

I took her arm, and we went off to find the ladies' room inside the restaurant. We were steps away from the entrance when she stopped, plopped down on a row of empty chairs lined up just outside the door, and passed out. Her eyes rolled back. She was having a small seizure.

"Mom? *Mom? Mom!*" I screamed.

I looked over to see Bella standing by the table in the corner of the patio. She was on her cell phone.

"Mom!" I yelled, still trying to snap her out of it.

At the table right in front of us, a nurse and a doctor were having lunch with their friends. They stood up, laid her down on the row of chairs, and shooed me away. Bella, along with many others, called 911 before the doctor yelled for someone to do so. It took forever for the ambulance to arrive, something the doctor and nurse were quite upset about. While we waited, we learned that the ambulance got stuck in drawbridge traffic, more information that upset the doctor and the nurse. But finally, off she went to the local hospital.

"Are you her daughter?" one of the EMTs asked.

"Yes," I replied.

"What hospital would you like her to go to?"

"I have no idea."

"How about Mercy South? That's the closest," the EMT informed me.

"Is it a good hospital?"

"Yes."

"Would you send your mother there?"

"Yes."

"OK then."

I wondered why I hadn't done any research on local hospitals and health-care facilities before an emergency took place and I had an EMT staring me in the face.

Bella and I met the ambulance at the hospital, which was located in the middle of a large medical community. We spoke with my mother; she seemed fine, so I went out to speak with the doctor on call.

"She hallucinates," I informed him. I jumped at the opportunity to introduce her history, particularly the hallucinations.

"Oh?" he replied.

"Yes. She hasn't been herself lately, and I've been trying to figure out what's going on."

"That's good to know. I'll make a note in her chart."

I was relieved to finally be able to disclose my concerns to a real-live Florida doctor.

Mom was in the emergency room for hours while they ran initial tests. She was assigned to Nurse Freespirit. She was stylish, young, and pretty, and had long, curly hair, but after a brief five minutes, Bella and I quietly wondered if she was having a very bad day. It's not uncommon for a nurse to have a difficult time inserting an IV, or finding supplies, or getting machines to work, or staying focused enough to ask pertinent questions, but it *is* uncommon to have all these scenarios play out at the same time with the same nurse. Mom's alarms kept going off, and after a while, Nurse Freespirit would come in casually and appear to be angry at my mother for making them go off and disrupting what she was doing. The alarm went off a number of times, with Nurse Freespirit returning, huffing and puffing until, aha! She spied Bella's pocketbook, a cute little designer piece with an exclusive name that I had never heard of. It was then that she categorically opted to spend more time doting on Bella—I mean my mother. No, actually I do mean Bella, telling her stories about herself like they had been best friends forever. She was talking about her sex life, her kids, how Moroccan oil was expensive but great on her hair, and something about a gas station that I didn't understand (but did know was terribly inappropriate). Her behavior was so bizarre that Bella and I kept glancing at each other, questioning her actions with our eyes.

Time moves slowly while you sit powerlessly in the ER with your loved one, but it moves on nonetheless.

"Peggy, I really have to go," groaned Bella.

She'd stayed much longer than she should have, as she had another commitment. But she'd picked us up and brought us to the restaurant, so her leaving meant me leaving, which meant leaving Mom alone with Nurse Freespirit. It's never easy making the decision to go and leave a loved one in the hospital, but sadly, eventually it just needs to be done. So Bella (the fearless little peanut we all love dearly but are just a little afraid of) addressed Nurse Freespirit with her best authoritative voice. "Look, this is my favorite auntie Francesca." (As if she had more than one auntie Francesca!) "We have to leave here, but we really don't want to, so I'll tell you what: you promise to take great care of her, and I'll buy you a pocketbook just like mine, and I'll get you some Moroccan oil too."

"Wow! Yes, I promise to treat her like a queen!" exclaimed Nurse Freespirit.

And with that not-so-convincing statement, we left.

Later that evening, I called the hospital to check in and see how Mom was doing.

"How are you, Mama?" I asked.

"This friggin' good-for-nothing nurse! My alarms keep going off, and she just keeps walking by and ignoring me," she fumed.

"Really?"

What happened to the bribery deal? I thought.

"She came in once to stop the alarm and yelled at me, like I'm doing it on purpose!"

At this point in the journey with my mother, I never knew what to believe as truth and what was made up in her mind, so I took her accusations with a grain of salt.

"Maybe you should just try to get some sleep," I said.

"How can I sleep? I haven't eaten all day."

"Why don't you ask Nurse Freespirit for something to eat?"

"I did. She gave me a chicken salad sandwich, but these damn alarms keep going off, and she won't come in to turn them off. She just keeps ignoring me. How can I eat with all this noise?"

"Are you still in the same room in the ER?"

"Yes."

The emergency room was not like any ER I had ever had the pleasure to visit. It looked more like the medical center that surrounded it. The nurses' station was in the center of a very large room with cubicles, desks, and file cabinets. One exterior wall had individual and double patient rooms that had glass walls from floor to ceiling, enabling anyone at the station to see all the patients at all times.

"I keep waving at her to come into the room, but she just ignores me," she said.

"I can't believe she's ignoring you," I replied, thinking about the bribe Bella made with Nurse Freespirit.

"Yeah, well, I finally got her attention."

"What did you do?"

"I threw my chicken salad sandwich out of the room."

"You what?"

"I threw the chicken salad sandwich out of the room."

"You threw your chicken salad sandwich? Out to the nurses' station?"

"Yes, I did. Hey, I finally got her attention,"

As I envisioned gobs of chicken salad all over the floor, waiting for someone to clean it up, I was conflicted with feelings of guilt for not being there and relief that she was well enough to fight and throw things. I was hesitant to push the story any further, but my curiosity got the best of me.

"What happened to the chicken salad sandwich?"

"Nothing. My roommate ate it."

"*What*? Mom! What do you mean your roommate ate it? How could she eat a chicken salad sandwich after you threw it across the floor?"

"It was fine. It was in a package; you know, like you would get from a vending machine."

The next morning, Bella called me to see how her favorite auntie Francesca was doing. I told her the story of Nurse Freespirit ignoring her and the alarms and the chicken salad sandwich being thrown out of the room.

"That's it! No pocketbook for Nurse Freespirit or oil for her long, curly hair," Bella professed.

When I got to the hospital, my mother was resting comfortably in her room. I was told that she had had a vasovagal response and that they would be running numerous tests over the next two or three days to make sure she was in fact physically fit. She certainly appeared to be. I was among many who marveled at my mother's beauty and her perfectly fit form.

"Was she a professional dancer?" asked many health-care professionals tending to her.

"No, but she walks daily and eats healthy food," I replied.

The hospital cardiologist came by to see us around noon. I followed him out of Mom's room and met him in the hallway. Anxious to plead my case before he ran off to another patient, I blurted out, "She has hallucinations, and I'm concerned about her behavior."

"We haven't found anything wrong medically," he said in a very apathetic manner.

He was a small, tidy man with a sterile appearance and a monotone voice, who wore a white lab coat with his name embossed in blue on the breast pocket. He avoided looking into my eyes. I was worried he was disinterested.

Maybe he just needs more information, I thought.

"But I'm telling you, something is very wrong," I desperately pleaded.

"She hallucinates because she drinks too much," he said assuredly yet dispassionately.

How did he reach that conclusion? I thought. I was stunned.

"She doesn't drink very much at all. She does have a glass of wine about five times a week, but it's just one glass—never two," I insisted.

"Of course that's what she'd tell you."

"No, actually I see it. She lives with me. She drinks about a bottle of wine a week."

"She can still hide her drinking from you."

"No, honestly, sometimes two glasses, but only on special occasions. She hallucinates, and she's frightened because she sees men in her home, gunfire, cars chasing her, and people trying to kill her."

"I'm sure when you go home, you will find empty vodka bottles under her bed." He wore his indifference like an expensive new suit.

I stood there silent and stunned, realizing why he preferred to look at the shiny mint-green floor that matched the walls instead of into my eyes.

"Look, I can have her committed to the psych ward and they can test her there if you'd like," he said as he initiated his escape.

"I don't want to have her committed. I want someone to help me figure out what's going on with her," I said to his back as he walked away.

Left with the agony of abandonment, I stood in that shiny mint-green hallway alone, watching him turn the corner out of my sight. I wanted him to talk with me. Maybe I would have agreed to a psychological evaluation as a course of action to find a diagnosis, but I certainly couldn't agree to have her committed and surrender to his alcoholic theory.

Later that day, her primary care physician came in to check on her.

Yes! I thought. *Another chance! Finally, I was going to see the doctor I wrote to, not once, but twice, with concerns about my mother.* I was sure he'd done some research and would shed some light on her behavior. Maybe he'd even have a diagnosis.

"How are you feeling?" Dr. Primary Care Number One asked my mother.

"I feel fine," she replied.

"Well, everything looks good," he said. "Can I see you outside in the hallway?" he asked me five seconds later. He had spent less than three minutes with her.

"Yes," I said, thinking his bedside manner needed some polishing.

"You sent me a letter?"

"Yes, I'm worried about my mother. She's hallucinating."

"Oh?"

"It's been going on for a while now. I don't know what's wrong with her."

He looked at me pensively for a few moments. "OK, thank you," he said. Then he turned and walked away.

Another doctor left me standing in the shiny hallway, stunned and alone, trying to process the situation.

"Am I going to die?" Mom asked when I returned to her room.

"No, of course not."

"What's wrong?"

"Honestly Mom, I don't know. And neither does he."

~

I left after dinner and went home to process the day. I sat outside in the warm tropical air, appreciating the cool ocean breeze that came by every now and then to kiss the back of my neck. Neighbors my mother once considered friends stopped by, pleased to have the opportunity to re-veal enlightening stories. They took turns telling me they were sincerely concerned about my mother's bizarre behavior. They added that she was becoming reclusive and skittish. They told stories about her anger, of her yelling at people in the shared laundry room. They talked about how she ran out of her condo to her male friend and protector across the street; she would sometimes knock on his door or hide in his shrubbery. But their biggest concern was about how much time Mom spent inside the condo and how little she spent out in the fresh air.

I hoped day two at the hospital was going to be much more productive. I requested a meeting with the neurologist who was running tests, and I was assured she would see me that day. I practically wore a pathway in the shiny linoleum while walking between Mom's room and the nurses' station. My short experience with this facility left me dubious, even though the gatekeeper assured me the doctor was close by and promised to tell her I was eager to see her.

"I'm just checking in," I said to the nurse behind the counter.

"Oh no! She just left. There she goes—down the hall," she said.

"Excuse me! Excuse me, Dr. Neurologist," I shouted while running toward her. I didn't even have time to acknowledge how annoyed I felt.

She stopped to address me. "How can I help you?"

"I wanted to talk with you about my mother."

"Who's your mother?"

"Francesca. There is something wrong with her, and I need help."

Dr. Neurologist wore the same white lab coat with her name embossed in blue on the breast pocket, but hers wasn't nearly as crisp and white as Dr. Cardiologist's coat. She seemed tired and a bit disheveled, but she had a kind face and didn't seem to mind looking at my face when she addressed me. I was pleased. She looked like the kind of person I could relate to. Then she spoke. "Hey, I like to have a cocktail or two myself."

Tears instantly formed as my eyes met with hers. *Oh my God, she drank Dr. Cardiologist's Kool-Aid*, I thought in defeat.

"Listen, we have done everything we can here. All her tests came back fine. There is nothing wrong with her from a neurological standpoint."

I couldn't breathe.

"The vein in her neck—"

I could feel myself getting panicky.

"No physical signs of anything that would cause her to hallucinate. No blockage, no—"

I stood motionless as the conversation swirled around in my head, not making any sense, until I went completely numb.

I heard the sound of the elevator door open and watched as it swallowed her up whole. I didn't get a rebuttal. I wasn't given the opportunity to ask a question. The elevator doors shut. She was gone. Once again, I went home to New England with no answers.

Shortly after that hospital stay, Mom changed her primary care physician. Dr. Primary Care Number Two came with a brilliant recommendation as being a great listener who was also thoughtful, kind, and thorough. I had renewed optimism for a working relationship with someone in the medical field who was absolutely going to get to the bottom of Mom's condition. I had facts, recorded data, history, and research. I had time to think and process her hospital stay and wondered if the reason the doctors at Mercy South dismissed me so quickly was because Mom had had too much to drink the night before. I could have explained that to them if I was given the chance. I was hopeful that Dr. Primary Care Number Two and I would work together and really make some headway. I allowed myself to hope for a working relationship with Dr. Primary Care Number Two that included phone calls and scheduled visits to Florida. I was ready.

Excited about Mom's change in venue, I wrote Dr. Primary Care Number Two a letter stating that I was her daughter and she had lived with me for many years. I detailed that I'd witnessed her behavior first-hand and on a daily basis, as well as describing her excruciating hallucinations, fictitious stories, and her ability to mask her symptoms. I told Dr. Primary Care Number Two that I'd taken my mother to my doctor in New England the previous August, who agreed she needed follow-up attention. I wrote about how upon returning home, I got the familiar finger in my face as Mom told me to leave it alone as she refused follow-up treatment. Months went by.

I never heard a word from Dr. Primary Care Number Two.

Mom's phone calls were becoming agonizingly troublesome. In fact, they became all-consuming. She was petrified and would flee from her bed and from her home. She called me constantly. Left again to my own devices, I started reviewing everything I had learned. I had exhausted the medical community, ruled out prescribed medication's side effects, and proved her stories false, so I went back to the elderly schizophrenia theory I'd had earlier. It was obvious I wasn't able to help her, and at that point, I was questioning whether anyone could—or would. But I kept researching, kept talking about it to anyone who would listen, kept engaging in her painful phone calls, and became completely immersed in her distress.

My daughter-in-law suggested I contact her sister, who had just earned a PhD in neuropsychology and was actively working in New York City at a prestigious hospital. She asked questions, consulted with colleagues, asked follow-up questions, and gave me great feedback. It was the first time I felt a sincere interest from someone in the medical community with knowledge of the elderly brain. We exchanged a number of lengthy e-mails before she finally called me. "Peggy, I really don't think your mother has elderly schizophrenia," she professed.

"Well, do you have any other ideas of what could be wrong?" I asked.

"I don't. But I did talk with a number of people, and they all agree it doesn't sound like schizophrenia."

"What do you suggest I do?"

"You should have her evaluated by a neurologist."

"I'll try. I just don't know how. She's capable of making her own decisions, and she thinks she's fine."

"I'm so sorry. It's a difficult situation, but she does have a right to decline help."

I thought about Dr. Cardiologist and the lost opportunity to have her evaluated.

Completely disheartened, I simply stopped trying for a couple of months. I took to the couch for comfort until Tom reached out to a friend for some help. Barbara is a nurse who had worked in nursing homes, both as a nurse and as an administrator, for many years. She made a phone call and spoke with my mother to see if she could make any inferences through a conversation. She called Mom and spoke with her for twenty minutes.

"She's a little off, but I didn't hear any signs of dementia," Barbara told me.

"Did she talk about the people trying to kill her?" I asked.

"No, she didn't, but I did have a long conversation with her, asked a lot of questions, and she followed right along."

"Any thoughts?"

"No, I'm sorry. I know this is hard on you, but I really don't know what to tell you."

"Thanks for trying, Barbara."

"Another medical professional with plenty of empathy and no answers," I said to Tom after I hung up the phone.

He starred at me sympathetically, unable to respond.

"I don't understand. She's worked with the elderly all her adult life. She's never seen this behavior before?"

"I don't know what to tell you, Peggy. It's baffling."

~

When Mom returned to New England for her summer 2011 stay, I was pretty despondent. She was still proficient with managing to hide her symptoms from everyone up north except Tom and me. I continued to dwell on how I could get her evaluated. "Mom, why don't you make me your health care proxy?" I argued.

"No, I don't need one," she insisted.

"Everyone needs a health care proxy and an advocate."

"Well, if that's true, I certainly don't want it to be you. If something is wrong with me, you'll tell the whole world."

"How about one of the boys then?"

"No, I don't want anyone to be my advocate."

"I wish I could force you, but I can't."

"No, you can't."

As close as we were, we were two very different people, and she knew it. I liked to share with others; Mom liked to sweep things under the rug. But every day what I heard from my mother was "Help me—no, don't help me—Help me; but not *that* way—Help me; play the lottery—help me; no, never mind; I'm fine!"

She may have been able to convince herself *she* was fine, but I was not fine, not fine at all, and I was desperate to find answers, support, and resources. Maybe she didn't want any help, but I needed some for my well-being.

One morning, Tom dragged me out of the house for the day. We left before Mom woke at her typical ten o'clock hour, so I asked my neighbor to check in on her during the day. Alicia has been my neighbor for over thirty years. Our boys grew up together and remain close to this day. Alicia had lost her mother many years earlier, so she adopted my mother as a surrogate. They would go on long walks together and chat through the entire jaunt. She thought the world of Mom, and Mom trusted her in return, which was huge. Trust was not something my mother gave away freely. I thought it was safe asking Alicia to be the one to check in on her, although in the back of my mind, I knew that anyone knocking on the door would be troublesome for Mom.

When we returned, Mom was sitting at the kitchen table in her seat of choice fighting with her checkbook, and she was *furious*! "Where did you go?" she asked curtly.

"We had to run some errands," I responded.

I could feel her staring at me as I went about the kitchen, so I turned to face her and stared back. She abruptly got up, went upstairs to her room, and I went to mine where I sat and stewed.

This is what it comes down to? I'm in my midfifties, survived raising three boys and all their friends; managed to stay married through raising three boys and all their friends; still have a roof over my head and my sanity; and now I can't go out with my husband for a couple of hours because my mother can't be left alone? I could understand if she couldn't be left alone because she might burn the house down or needed physical care. But the thoughts of having to stay home to tend to her psychological needs when the whole rest of the world—including multiple doctors and a hospital—insisted that there wasn't anything wrong with her so I must be the crazy one was just infuriating! Every fiber of my being screamed, "Would someone *please* tell me how to make sense of this agonizing situation?"

And the world replied, "Situation? What situation?"

It was that summer that my mother stopped helping out around the house. She had slowed down a little bit the summer before, but that seemed like a natural progression. That summer, she stopped completely. It took everything she had just to tend to her own personal needs.

"What's with your mother? She doesn't even unload the dishwasher anymore," Tom asked.

"Something's seriously wrong, Tom. Surely you know that," I answered.

"I understand, but she's always been good about helping out."

"Don't you think if she could, she would?" Hearing the words come out of my mouth reinforced that realization for me. Even as I was defending her, I had the same thoughts.

"Yeah. I guess you're right," Tom agreed.

Thinking about it broke my heart. All my life, I rarely saw Mom sit down. She believed the world offered many opportunities to get exercise for free and be useful at the same time.

"Why does anyone need to pay to go to a gym when there's so much to do around the house?" she would ask.

"You're right, but people like the gym." The thought made me giggle.

"If you want to lift weights, go stack some wood."

"Not everyone has a woodpile," I said, trying to get her to see another point of view.

"There are always things to pick up off the floor, which is good for getting your stomach in shape—or you could go for a walk. There are so many productive things you can do to stay in shape! Vacuum, rake leaves."

That was her lifelong mantra, and she followed it faithfully. When she stopped following it, I knew something was terribly wrong—not just psychologically, but physically as well, adding one more piece to the puzzle.

She stopped doing many things she had enjoyed in the past. She loved to read autobiographies; she thought novels were a waste of time. My father read novels all the time and sometimes reread the same one without realizing it until he was halfway through. She saw reading fiction as a way to avoid work, so she didn't read very often, but when she did, she loved to read about real-life drama. With her slowing down physically and spending more time in her room, I looked for a good book for her to get into. I found a publication about Elizabeth Taylor that had just been released and proudly brought it to her while she was up in her room. Two days later, she gave the book back to me.

"Why don't you want to read the book?" I contested.

"I already know the story," she informed me.

"But you love Elizabeth Taylor." I stood quietly, trying to understand her motive. But when I opened my mouth to ask another question, she dismissed me by leaving the room to return to hers. She didn't want to explain.

Later that evening, I went up to check on her and saw she was reading a book by Shel Silverstein. It was a children's book that she found among some things left behind by my boys. My heart sank, and my legs went limp. The big book about Elizabeth Taylor was more than she could handle. She was reading children's books to keep her brain active. She instinctively did whatever she could to keep her mind functioning and strong. She was fighting so hard and chose to fight it alone. Was this new action cognitive behavior or instinctual? Did she know that her brain was clogging up and cutting off small pieces of what once made her Francesca? Was she really only capable of reading at an elementary level? Did she know my heart was breaking?

A new piece of the puzzle, I thought as I turned to go back downstairs, unnoticed.

EIGHT

Finally

MY MOTHER'S MOTHER was the cog that held the family wheel together. Everyone who was related to my grandmother and her fifteen children felt blessed to be a part of this loud, wonderful family. Marriages and children were abundant. Some moved away from the town they grew up in, and some stayed behind, becoming the cog that kept everyone close at heart. Grandma couldn't be more pleased with her extra-large family.

"Where did you get that ring, Grandma?" I asked one evening while she was sitting at our kitchen table having coffee. She was sporting a gigantic plastic diamond ring, and she was showing it off with great glee.

"I got it at the concert hall," she replied.

"For what?"

"Carol Channing was asking people how many grandchildren they had. Some people were shouting out 'ten!' and some said, 'twenty!' I think someone even said 'twenty-five.'"

"Grandma, that's so funny. What did you do?"

"I raised my hand and said 'seventy-six.'"

I burst into laughter.

"They brought me up on the stage. Oh, Carol Channing couldn't believe it," she said.

"So you won the prize?"

"Of course I did! People can't get over how many of us we are," she said, beaming.

My grandmother was the center of our world. The family members who moved away often returned to her home for a visit, a dish of macaroni, or a bowl of homemade soup. After she passed away, three of Mom's sisters inherited the role, keeping abreast of what was going on with everyone in the family. While their love and commitment to my mother and me was unwavering, much needed, and greatly appreciated, the distance didn't allow for them to be as involved as any of us would have liked. They did their best to help me with Mom's problems, but they were busy taking care of Auntie Mae, who had sold her restaurant and moved closer to her sisters. She had symptoms similar to Mom's, but hers were far more advanced.

In addition to having the close proximity of her sisters to help, Auntie Mae welcomed the service of a number of doctors and allowed her sisters to advocate for her. Mom, on the other hand, avoided medical intervention and wouldn't discuss her symptoms and fears with anyone, including her doctor. She refused my pleas to arrange appointments around the time when I was able to accompany her. She put a giant wall up around herself, and she wasn't going to let anyone knock it down.

~

Midsummer came along, and my mother began to think about returning to Florida. I was worried and did my best to avoid any conversation around the subject. I wanted her to stay with me in New England, at least long enough to get her diagnosed and treated.

"I really need to go back to Florida," she said.

"I don't think you should go," I replied.

"Peggy, I'm fine, and I'm going back to Florida."

"Please, Mom, please stay so we can figure out what's going on with you."

"Nothing is wrong with me. I'm fine."

"But what about all the people trying to kill you?"

"They're trying to kill me here too."

"But you'll be safe with me," I pleaded.

"I won't be safe anywhere, so I may as well be warm."

For years, I booked her trips because she was no longer capable of using the computer. She couldn't get beyond the messages on the screen that people were sending her about some conspiracy that ultimately forced her off the computer with threats of harming her children and grandchildren if she didn't do as she was told. Most of the time, it had to do with my brother Tim or my son Matthew, who were often overseas on a ship.

"Are you going to book my trip?" she asked again.

"I don't think you should go to Florida, Mom." I struggled with emotions, swinging between feeling like a small child crying for her mommy to stay home and feeling like I was her mother, trying to keep her safe.

"I have to go," she said.

I was dazed and conflicted.

"I have things I need to do there," she said as she stormed off.

She booked her own flight the old-fashioned way—with a land line and a credit card.

With Mom back in Florida, I called her doctor's office and pleaded with them to have Dr. Primary Care Number Two call me as soon as possible. I gave the office my cell phone number. From that moment on, I clung to my phone and didn't let it out of my sight for one tiny minute. Someone had to diagnose her, and at that point, I was determined it would have to be her Florida doctor. Days later, I was sitting in a restaurant with my friend Lizzy when the call finally came. I ran outside to give the long-awaited conversation my complete attention, hoping for some answers.

"I received and read your letter," said Dr. Primary Care Number Two.

"Something is terribly wrong with my mother," I said as I stood outside in the freezing rain.

"I sympathize with you, but I did an Alzheimer's test on her and found no reason for concern."

"She's hallucinating very badly. I need help. I don't know what to do."

"I spoke with your mother. She said she's fine and doesn't need help. I have to honor that."

"What am I supposed to do?"

"I don't know. I don't know if you can do anything."

"What about when she starts talking irrational and becomes delusional? Can you help me with that?"

"What do you mean?"

"Well, how do I handle her—how do I talk to her when she's not making any sense?"

"With all due respect, you *can't* talk to a crazy person." In retrospect, I'm sure she was doing the best she could but I didn't see that. I needed more. I needed someone to listen to my story.

As I stared off into the cold, dark night, trying to process that statement, I couldn't find any words. I took too long to respond, giving the doctor enough time to end the conversation. Another missed opportunity to help this wonderful woman who sacrificed all her life for others. *Shame on you*, I thought as I walked back into the restaurant. *She's a wonderful human being. Shame on all of you.*

Trying to help Mom from a distance was maddening. I spent every free moment contemplating what I was doing wrong. Everywhere I went, I watched mothers and daughters interacting. One day while sitting alone in my doctor's office, I prayed for answers. As I stared off into space, I heard a daughter explaining the outcome of the visit to her mother. "All set to go, Mom?" the younger woman asked.

"Do I have a new medication?" the older woman inquired.

"Yes, but don't worry; I'll be right here to help."

I wanted so much to have that relationship with my mother. We were so close that neither of us made a move without the other knowing, yet when it came to her illness, we could not be further apart. I felt like the lone woman having difficulties conceiving a baby and sitting at the OB-GYN office with pregnant women all around her.

"You're so lucky to have that relationship with your mom," I said to the younger woman.

"Thank you," she replied.

"My mother fights me tooth and nail."

"I'm sorry. That makes it hard."

"It does."

I wanted to cry, but I didn't have the energy.

~

For fifteen years, I worked at a neighborhood church. I started out part time in the office while raising my family and going to school two nights a week, working toward a bachelor's degree in psychology. After graduating in 1999, I took the job of director of religious education while still maintaining the office duties. It was a wonderful place to work, and I loved every minute of it. My boss, my colleagues, as well as the children in the program and their parents provided me with opportunities to flourish personally and professionally. During my employment at the church, I attended special-needs workshops and National Catholic Education conferences all around the country. I also earned a master of science degree. In the spring of 2011, I left the job at the end of the school year. Two years earlier a new administration had come in, bringing with it new rules and a different persona. Throughout this time, I was distracted by my mother's issues and had a difficult time coping with the changes. Things were said, feelings were hurt, and bonds were broken. Tom and I discussed the situation at great length and decided it was time for me to leave.

I really loved that job: my coworkers, the children, the environment, and the paycheck. Making that decision took weeks. It was agonizing, and it took away hours of sleep. With the accumulation of my mother's issues and the loss of my job, I felt like my whole world had blown apart. I cried for weeks, but God's plan was greater than mine, and with no job, no children at home, and a husband about to go out to sea, I had the opportunity to spend a full month in Florida with Mom.

On January 14, 2012, Tom dropped me off at the bus that would take me to the airport and then made his way over the bridge to board his ship. I flew out that day; he sailed the next. For me, having that much time to devote to my mother in Florida, just the two of us with few distractions, came not a moment too soon. Far too despondent to help from afar, I spent my days on the couch watching TV and avoiding life.

I was still unable to figure out what was happening or how to help my now-manic mother. She was almost always filled with fear, and her hallucinations progressed immensely. She was exhausted—the little kids in her home ran her ragged, women gave her a hard time, and men invaded her life. The compulsive Killer talk had diminished a bit but was replaced with stories of people in her condo trying to harm her and take over her home.

"George came over and checked the condo for me," she had said during one of our nightly phone conversations a few weeks earlier. George was the previous owner and knew where all the skeletons were hiding.

"What did he check it for?" I asked reluctantly.

"The men. They hide in that crawl space in the ceiling where all those wires are."

"Mom, a small mouse couldn't hide in that space."

"Well, they must be somewhere. I know that they watch me in the shower."

"How could anyone possibly see you in the shower? There's not even a window in the bathroom."

"They drilled a peephole in there."

It amazed me how her answers were quick, easy, and yet completely irrational.

"I've never seen a peephole."

"Well you can see it now."

I wanted to take the phone and bang it repeatedly on the kitchen counter. I wanted to run away to the highest mountain peak and scream my head off. I thought of all the times I wanted to slap her and yell, "Snap out of it!"

Frustration turned to joy when I first got to Florida. There was always a two-day grace period where Mom seemed to be her old self—the Mom

I missed, and as much as I longed for more, I wouldn't get it. We spent a lot of intimate time together in the first two weeks, and I realized my endless reasoning skills weren't working a bit. I was getting nowhere fast and found myself spending as little time in the house with her as possible. One afternoon I was sitting outside the condo enjoying the warm tropical air when I got a text from my cousin Gigi.

"Lewy body...Google it."

I knew exactly what she meant. Without a word, I knew that Gigi had spoken with her mother, who accompanied Auntie Mae to the doctor, and while they were there, the doctor mentioned the disease. I ran into the house to start my research—and I was completely blown away.

Lewy body dementia is a disease that occurs when abnormal deposits of a protein called alpha-synuclein form in the brain, creating changes that can lead to problems with movement, thinking, mood, and behavior. LBD is one of the most common causes of dementia, just behind Alzheimer's and vascular disease. The symptoms include:

- **Hallucinations**
  Yes, check, thank you (but I've seen that symptom before).
- **Fluctuations in cognitive ability, attention, and/or alertness**
  Hmmm, this would explain why she makes sense one minute and not a lick the next. Or why she is able to have an intelligent conversation about current events and then forget how to tie her shoes. Check.
- **Slowness of movement, rigidity, or difficulty walking**
  Mom had been unsteady for years but very careful so no one would know. Check.
- **Sensitivity to medications**
  Mom had always been extra sensitive to drugs but had trouble with everything she took over the last few years. Check.

- **Frozen stance**
  Oh my goodness, that explains why she stares out the window absolutely motionless for fifteen minutes at a time. Definite check. My heart started racing as I continued to read.
- **Problems with balance, stooped posture, loss of coordination**
  Check.
- **Difficulty swallowing**
  She gave up eating rice. Check.
- **Lack of interest in daily activities, less social interaction**
  Let's weed out those friends. Check.
- **Delusions, strongly held false beliefs, or opinions not based on evidence**
  Oh my sweet Jesus! Check.
- **Paranoia in extreme**
  Absolutely check.
- **Irrational distrust of others, such as suspicion that people are taking and hiding things**
  A week ago, she told me that someone took her light bill and hid it until she finally found it under the kitchen table. Check.
- **Anxiety, intense apprehension, uncertainty and fear about future events or situations**
  So that's why she obsessed over upcoming events until she drove me out of my mind. Check.
- **Agitation, restlessness, irritability, pacing, and an inability to get settled**
  "Peggy, she's wandering." Check.
- **Changes in body temperature**
  Check.
- **Blood pressure issues, dizziness, fainting, and falling**
  Check, check, check, and check!

My mother had every single symptom on the lbd.org page with the exception of one—she didn't drool. From that point on, I *knew* she had

Lewy body disease, and no one was going to convince me otherwise. It was all there in black and white.

It was a long road getting to this realization. I spent well over a thousand days worrying about my mother, and as far as I was concerned, that was one thousand opportunities for anyone and everyone concerned to weigh in on the situation and help with solutions. That was it. I diagnosed her and was ready to suit up for battle—but I knew I would need help.

With ten days left of my visit to Florida, I managed to sneak in a phone call to her doctor's office. I told the woman on the phone what I'd learned and asked her to please find a reason to get her in the office while I was still there. I informed her of Mom's denial and that she would have a difficult time processing the information, and we would both need help with the next step. To her credit, they made the visit happen pretty quickly. With all the lemons that had been piling up in my bowl, I finally had a taste of sweet lemonade.

Mom told me that she would have to fast, as they intended to draw blood. It seemed to me rather unkind to schedule an afternoon appointment for someone who was fasting, but my mother did the planning, so I kept quiet. We waited in the office well over an hour to have the blood taken and another thirty minutes after that to get into a room. I brought crackers and water, which she ate after having her blood drawn, while still waiting to be seen. But by then it was almost three o'clock, and she hadn't eaten since the day before, so needless to say she was getting aggravated—and rightfully so. "This is ridiculous, Peggy; let's go!" she yelled.

"I know, but we've waited this long. We may as well wait another minute," I replied.

"I can't sit here any longer. It's been two hours."

I knew that while I didn't have a health-care proxy for her, the doctor would be able to share information with me if we were in the room together. I was sure they had information, a game plan, and resources for me. Time moved slowly as I anxiously waited.

"I don't want that surgery," Mom worried.

"On your brain?" I asked.

"Yes, you know, like Mae had where they drained the fluid from her brain."

"I know. I promise no brain surgery."

Auntie Mae had had a procedure where her neurologist drained some fluid out of her head to relieve pressure, hoping for improvement with motor skills, but it didn't help.

"And no more MRIs," she said.

"No more MRIs," I repeated. For once, an easy promise. I knew it wouldn't do anything to help her diagnosis.

It took everything I had to keep quiet while my mother gave false answers to her doctor, who kept glancing over to me to see me shake my head no. Just as my mother had predicted, there was talk of another MRI of the brain, the second one in two years.

"No more MRIs," I said softly. I was surprised the doctor suggested it.

"You know your daughter thinks you have Lewy body disease," said the doctor.

Mom stared, speechless.

"What do you think about that, Francesca?"

Mom continued to stare.

"Well, then, I don't know what else I can do for you."

Now both Mom and I stared, speechless, trying to process her last statement of finality and doom.

Do something, I screamed inside my head. *Say something!*

"Would you like a referral to a neurologist?" said Doctor Primary Care Number Two.

We were still staring when the doctor stood up abruptly and left the room without waiting another minute for an answer. Why did the doctor ask Mom what *she* wanted? Why didn't the doctor have a plan?

As I processed the procedures of that visit, the whole situation became incomprehensible. I left the office visit in slow motion. As we walked down the concrete hallway on the outside of the building, down the concrete steps, and into another concrete hallway that led us to the parking lot, I felt like I was pushing my body through that horrible concrete with each step. I was in a thick darkness, as though I was walking to my own funeral.

"Why do I need to see a neurologist? I just saw one last year," my mother said.

"I don't know, Mom," I said quietly.

How could I defend that statement? How could I have any reply at all if her own doctor couldn't reply? Didn't anyone else care about getting her a diagnosis? It was painfully obvious that I didn't have any credibility with her; we needed professional help! I left that office with every conceivable unhealthy emotion. After handing them a diagnosis on a silver platter, they discharged us in just fifteen minutes. We waited two and a half hours for fifteen minutes of nothing! I honestly didn't know what to do. I was in a constant state of panic, and once again, we were dismissed without resolve.

Now what?

I sat out the rest of the day and marched on the next morning. With knowledge comes strength and power. I heard the words of my friend Karen: "One foot in front of the other. Sometimes that's all you can do!" Then she would quickly follow with the best smile ever and add, "And that's OK—it's OK!"

I spent the remaining time in Florida taking babies, birds, and men out of her bed and protecting her from the women who were out to get her. She was a lot calmer when I was there to help with cooking, cleaning, and keeping her mind occupied. The isolation was too unsettling for her thought process, so I did whatever I could do to distract and entertain her. On the entertainment schedule was a planned trip to meet my soon-to-be daughter-in-law, Laura, and her dad, about thirty minutes away via highway. Mom's little Mustang was eighteen years old now, and according to her, "great for running around town; not so great on the highway." It took some convincing, but off we went.

We settled into a little café, on a small main street just off the high-way, that served gourmet pizzas. "What kind of pizza would you like, Mom?" I asked.

"I don't know, either the Margherita or the spinach and ricotta or the caramelized onion and fig," she said.

"I think I'll get a plain cheese," I said.

"Oh good, I'll have a bite."

The others ordered their pizza, and because I had already taken care of the bill with the waitress, I went ahead and ordered three pizzas for Mom and one more for me. We spent the next two and a half hours sharing pizza and catching up with stories. We made it home safely with half-eaten pizzas in to-go boxes, full bellies, and big smiles. The little old Mustang was a trooper and made the trek just fine. I was in the house packaging up the leftovers when Mom came in in a nervous huff. "Did you see that light on the dashboard of my car?" she asked.

"What light?" I inquired.

"The light that says we shouldn't have made that trip."

It wouldn't be unusual for my mother to see two words on a dash-board and relay her interpretation as a six-word warning; that would be the endearing quirkiness that we all got a kick out of, so I pushed on.

"But what did the light say?" I continued

"It says, you should not have made that trip—and it's blue."

"Ahhh," I said out loud. Now I was sure it was Lewy-speak. "I'll go look."

Just as I predicted, there weren't any lights on at all, with the excep-tion of the check engine light that had been continuously lit for at least ten years—and it was yellow, not blue. The irrational behavior that had haunted me for years now made sense. Having knowledge of the disease enabled me to have a completely different reaction.

"OK, Mom, we'll have the car checked out later this week," I said to take her mind off the current preoccupation and enable her to move on to something else.

Armed with information, I began to change my strategy. When we sat down at the kitchen table for lunch, I broached the subject.

"Mom, please come home with me so we can figure out what to do about the situation with the men invading your home," I begged.

"Absolutely not."

"But Mom, you can't call the police every minute of the day. They could Baker Act you."

"They know!" she said as if having knowledge of the weekly police meetings.

"They could put you in an institution."

She just stared at me with her piercing blue eyes.

"Do you understand what I'm saying?" I said.

"I have proof, Peggy. Why can't you see it?"

"That doesn't matter. You're scared here. You don't leave your home."

"I'll be all right. I've been doing this a long time."

"It's not healthy, Mom."

Sadly, I remembered the words a medical professional told me in an attempt to calm me down when I was upset about the situation: "Don't worry; if she's running around the streets of Florida half-naked, someone will call you!"

It didn't bring me any comfort then, but it would have to do for now.

~

Shortly after I got back to New England and Tom returned from sea, we went to Florida to check in on her. She had been asking us to replace a perfectly good doorknob for a couple of years, and Tom decided to do it on this visit, to put her at ease. With the new doorknob and deadbolt in place, she promptly sent me off to the hardware store to get four new sets of keys made, giving her motivation for her latest fixation. I had five sets made and gave one set to the condo manager without her knowledge. The manager had keys to every condo, with the exception of my mother's, as she flatly refused to give her a set. She didn't trust anyone to have a key, for fear they would pass it along to Killer. Previously I wasn't concerned with her holding it back, but in her present state, I thought it was imperative that someone I trusted be able to get into her home to check on her if she needed help.

"Peg, get some envelopes out of the desk," she insisted.

"How many?" I asked.

"Oh, about six."

"Here you go, Mom."

"OK, now write 'keys' on this one."

I honored her request but was annoyed that she didn't just do it herself.

She put a set of keys into the envelope.

"Now put this in the top drawer of your bureau," she ordered.

"OK. All safe," I replied.

"Now write 'keys' on these other three envelopes."

I did as I was told.

She proceeded to put keys in an envelope and then take them out and move them to a different envelope. I watched in awe and wondered what she was thinking. All the envelopes were the same. She moved the envelopes around from her desk to the kitchen table to the kitchen counter over and over again. Unable to figure out her thought process but pleased that she was occupied with a task, I left her with the keys and the envelopes and went for a walk. An hour later, I came back into the house to see envelopes ripped to pieces on the kitchen table. I went to check on the envelope in the top drawer of my bureau, and it was gone.

"What's going on?" I pushed.

"They're not right," she complained.

"What's not right?"

"Take this key off this ring and put it on that one over there. Now write 'keys' on this envelope," she added.

At that point, I knew I'd have no success in attempting to figure out her method or even trying to help. She continued her task of key labeling, ripping up of envelopes, and changing hiding places for hours and hours and days on end.

In the tiny condo, her struggle was as apparent as an elephant in the room. With nowhere to escape, Tom was uncomfortable, so I took action and put him to work. We cleaned up, went shopping, and started cooking. I made her soups, pasta sauces, and enough vegetables to supplement her now not-so-healthy regular eating habits, to get her through the next few months. If I couldn't get her to come home with me, at least I could stock up her freezer with some good food.

"Vitamins in a bowl," she said when I gave her a bowl of homemade soup.

"I'm glad you like it."

"I don't like to cook anymore." I wondered if she could.

"Well, I filled the freezer for you so you can eat up while I'm away."

NINE

*You have no right to expect people to help you just
because you need it.
People help from the heart.*

—Francesca Jean

Tom and I returned home to bask in the glow of our normal routine. We had been away for weeks, so we planned to just sit quietly and watch a couple of recorded episodes of *Downton Abbey*. Like an ostrich with its head in the sand, I wanted to hide my head in Tom's arms and pretend no one could see or touch me. I wanted to be in a safe, toasty-warm bubble where the outside world didn't exist. I wanted a break from my mother—for just one night! Tom lit a fire in the fireplace while I poured us each a glass of wine. We were curled up on the couch when the phone rang.

The caller ID told me it was Mom's neighbor in Florida. The ringing of the phone instantly popped my warm bubble, sending me to an upright position and preparing me for battle. I was immediately thrown back into reality. My reality of my mother's reality.

"Hi Peggy. It's Dina."

"What's going on?" I asked reluctantly.

"Your mom called the police. I called them over here to explain the situation, and they want to speak with you."

"Hello, ma'am," the police officer said.

"Hello," I replied.

"Your mother called us. She said there's been a man sleeping in her rocking chair for about a week now, and he won't leave. We didn't see anyone else in the home."

"I know. She hallucinates. Are you going to Baker Act her?"

"No, I don't think she's going to harm herself. As long as you're aware of the situation, but you really should do something about it soon."

"I will. Thank you."

After composing myself, I dialed her number. I was on the phone a few short minutes when I began to feel sick—not only heartsick, but physically sick.

"Mom, the police called me," I lamented.

"Everything is fine," she replied.

"Why did you call the police?"

"That man has been sleeping in my rocking chair all week."

"Oh Mom—"

"The police told him to go."

"The police officer said he didn't see anyone," I said, yet again hoping to bring her back to reality.

"Well, he's slippery. He comes and goes as he pleases."

"You're so careful with your keys. How could that be possible?"

"Wasn't that funny when the policeman said I have nice legs?" she said, giggling.

She was completely delusional. "Are you OK, Mom?"

"Remember, we saw him at that restaurant," she added. Making light of the situation was her favorite defense mechanism.

"Oh, Mom."

Our once-quiet, relaxing evening turned to a serious, gloomy discussion about the next phase of our lives. The time had come: she needed intervention. It was time to make arrangements, go get her, and bring her home permanently. It was an agonizing decision to make, as it would be life-changing for all of us and devastating for my mother when she finally figured it all out. I booked a flight for a few days away, still wondering if it was the right thing to do. Did she just have a bad day, or was she too tired to fight anymore?

The painful phone conversations over the next few days definitively answered those questions. She needed help.

"The man is still coming and sleeping in the chair, Peggy, and this time, he brought friends," she said during the next phone conversation.

"Did you open the door and let them in?" I asked.

"No, they must have magic keys because they are all in here."

"Mom, we checked all the keys. Remember?" I simply didn't know what to say.

"They come and go through the walls."

"What do you mean?"

"They must have lived here before because they can go from condo to condo without any windows or doors. They must have magic keys."

"Can you hold on a couple of days? I'm coming down."

"Peggy, I'm fine. If you could just get rid of these men, there wouldn't be any problems."

The next day she called me, which was unusual. I always called her because I had a long-distance calling plan. When she did call me, it was from her cell phone. I knew the drill. Don't answer the cell phone and call her right back on her land line. When I saw that she had called me from her land line, I knew she was frantic, so I prepared myself for more of the same. I was hoping she could keep it at bay as I counted off the days until my flight to get her. But she was in manic mode and just couldn't help herself. "Where did you go?" she asked.

"What do you mean, Mom?" I answered.

"You were here, but then you disappeared."

I closed my eyes and took a deep breath. I felt sick to my stomach.

"These women won't leave. Did you tell them they could stay here, because I didn't!"

"No, I didn't tell them they could be there. Do you want me to talk to them now?" I was sure she would be sane enough to recognize that they wouldn't be able to talk to me, but I was wrong.

"What? Now you don't want to talk to her?" she said.

I could see my mother, standing in her living room, holding the phone out to her hallucinations, waiting for one of them to take it from her.

I closed my eyes and went numb.

~

The minute I arrived in Florida, my mother behaved as if nothing ever happened. She was happy to see me for sure, but she also realized that complaining about strange people in her house would prompt a conversation about her living with me full time, and she definitely did not want that. She'd be OK coming north with me a couple of months early, but she absolutely planned to return to Florida in the fall. I was pretty confident she would not. For the past few years, she'd worked very hard at masking her symptoms, and she tried concealing them again on the night of my arrival, but it didn't last long. I took seven babies, two men, three women, a bird, and a cat out of her bed.

That was when I established my next lifeline, my most-adored text buddy. The ability to text and have my friend respond quickly was a godsend for me. I spent a lot of time alone with my mother, especially when we were in Florida. As normalcy started to diminish and I exhausted every possible avenue I could think of to communicate the situation to her or with her, I desperately needed to find a channel to sanity. Yet I couldn't pick up the phone and talk with someone, because she was always within earshot, and I didn't want to offend her by running out of the house every time I was frustrated. I would look as irrational as she was, running in and out of the house every two minutes because I was constantly frustrated. The isolation I felt while in Florida was often unbearable, so texting became my outlet to the sane outside world. It was instantaneous, confidential, and helped me stay connected.

My Tom fit the earth angel role on so many levels, but texting wasn't one of them. For one thing, although he will unequivocally deny it, he doesn't always hear his phone. For another, he felt like he had to fix every issue or have a sensible answer for every off-the-wall situation. He wanted to belabor each individual scenario until he came up with a sensible solution. He was my warrior and protector. But for me, nothing made sense, and all the trying in the world hadn't changed that fact. I wanted to rant, vent, think bad thoughts, say bad things, and pray for forgiveness before I went to sleep at night. I struggled with the "crazy" task all day long. At the end of the day, all I wanted to do was complain, laugh, and breathe. So I reached out to my friend Lizzy, my sanity saver. Lizzy and I have been friends for forty years. We raised our husbands and children together. We had a business together. We leaned on each other for physical and emotional support. And we never had one single argument. We just clicked.

I began texting:

> Hey, I need a text buddy.
> 7:56
> Just need to bombard you with random Lewy speak and don't expect any responses.
> 7:59
> Just need to send them off.
> 7:59
> Can you handle it?
> 8:00
> Tom doesn't qualify because he feels like he has to respond and make sense out of things.
> 8:05
> Help!!!
> 8:06

I was behaving a little manic myself.
Lizzy responded.
I'm here sista…text away!!!
8:11

Lizzy was the perfect choice. She could sense when I needed a hello, and boom, a comforting text would appear with a whole bunch of bright pink hearts attached. I was enamored with her emoji capabilities. Lizzy knew when to reply with humor, when to be more serious, and when to reply with sympathy. She could sense when she needed to drop the text and make a person-to-person call on the phone. She was, hands-down, always there for me.

> I'm chasing invisible people out of her bed and house
> but she's really upset because this guy dropped
> off a bird and he has no right to. And now it's in her bed.
> 8:20
> She said she doesn't understand. She was so happy here
> but now these people are here and it's not fair.
> 8:30

I'm sorry Peg.
8:31

> I carried the babies out of the bed but there's still a
> bird. I told her I didn't see a bird and she said
> well I can see the feathers.
> 8:32

Tell her birds are good luck. They symbolize flying
like the plane ride home. The birds are a sign that she
is going somewhere. They are there to help with the journey.
8:33

> Pray. I just have to get her home. She could and would
> fool you. She only tells me about it. Now she's worried about
> getting bird flu!
> 8:40

Oh God Peg, you poor thing. Are you sure she can fly home?
8:41
I wasn't sure.

We spent the next four days preparing the condo for a long vacancy. I did the preparing while she gave instructions, supervised, and scrutinized. We left the fourth day for bathroom preparations and getting ready for travel.

Day One: Monday

We drove to the grocery store to get a few things, including cold cuts for travel sandwiches, fresh fruit, and cream for coffee. We planned to consume whatever was in the freezer and refrigerator, so I didn't need to buy much. Then we drove over to the other side of town to pick up a car cover and one more stop for lottery tickets. When we were through with our errands and returned to the condo, she quickly got out of the car.

"Now back it in," she ordered. I had taken over the Florida driving two years earlier, as Mom had difficulty reaching the pedals.

My first attempt was crooked, my second try was too far to the right, my third was too far to the left, fourth was crooked again, fifth was too far to the right again, sixth was still too far to the right, seventh was now too far to the left, eighth was still too far to the left, ninth was crooked, tenth was still crooked, and the eleventh? *I didn't care.*

"It's staying here, or you can do it yourself," I barked.

She opted for the former, as she knew she wouldn't be able to do any better, but she wasn't too pleased with me. We covered the car, and then I made dinner, cleaned up, and took the rest of the night off.

Day Two: Tuesday

Mom made coffee while I spent an hour on my computer. I went for a late-morning walk, came back, and made lunch. We spent the afternoon throwing things out, putting things in storage, playing hide the keys, making an early dinner, and scrubbing the kitchen.

"Now we need to clean and unplug the refrigerator," she demanded.

"But we're going to be here for two more days!"

"I can't put that off until the last minute. It'll have to settle for a few days. After you unplug the refrigerator, it might leak."

"I just bought it last year. It's brand new. It will be easy to clean, and it won't leak, I promise."

"Peggy, we can't wait."

"Yes we can! Look how easy this is." Within a minute, I pulled the refrigerator away from the wall, unplugged it, and plugged it back in.

"I've done this a million times. I know what needs to be done," she said in an angry tone.

"But what about food and ice?" I kept trying.

"Peggy, we're done. I'm unplugging it now."

"That's ridiculous." I was so mad I couldn't see straight.

"I'm not arguing with you." She didn't care how mad I was. She was going to get her way.

I dropped the subject and went about my business, giving her a few minutes to reconsider her way of thinking and at least listen to my mine, something she would have done in the past. Not five minutes later, she made it perfectly clear that wasn't happening.

"Are you going to unplug that refrigerator or shall I?" she asked.

"Mom, please. Trust me, I will deal with the refrigerator." I gave it one more try.

"Nope. I'll do it then."

I thought about her illness. I thought about all the sacrifices she made for me. I told myself the food would be OK for one more day. I kept my eyes on the prize, and that was getting her home, so I calmed down and acquiesced. "All right, we'll make it through the night if we leave the doors closed."

"We can't leave the doors closed," she said.

"What do you mean? That's preposterous," I replied, watching my composure fly out the window.

"The doors have to stay open."

"When we leave, maybe, but not two days before."

"*Stop!* Stop telling me how to do this. I'm the one that closes this place up every year. I know how it's done, not you!" She was now at a screaming level.

"It's a new refrigerator!" I screamed back. "You don't know what you're talking about!"

I couldn't believe how unreasonable she was, and she couldn't understand why I didn't just follow her rules. We were both too upset to continue. I gave in before we both had heart attacks.

We had one tiny cooler that was about five inches by six inches by seven inches, and the car was unavailable, making it impossible to make a store run. I packed up some cold cuts and yogurt, gave what I could to a neighbor, and threw everything else out. I then made myself a good stiff drink and sat outside, texting Lizzy. I was so upset with my mother I didn't trust myself to stay in the same room with her.

Day Three: Wednesday

We ate toast and apples for breakfast, ham-and-cheese sandwiches for lunch (with no mustard, because we had to throw it away), ham-and-cheese sandwiches with no mustard for dinner, and warm bottled water. We stayed busy packing our own bags and kept out of each other's way. She continued on with her duty, pleased that she got her way, and I remained irritated for not getting mine.

Day Four: Thursday

It was our travel day.

We ate toast and apples for breakfast, and I was unquestionably cranky while I did the last-minute cleaning. With the car we reserved to pick us up only ten minutes away, it was time to tackle the toilet. The condo was tiny, and the bathroom was no exception. I (of course) had the task of putting plastic wrap over the toilet, the "out of order" sign on top of the plastic wrap, and another "out of order" sign on the seat. My mother (of course) had to stand over me telling me how to do it, how I was doing it wrong, that I needed to use more tape, and where I missed a spot. I was sweating, claustrophobic, hungry, and cranky. I couldn't take another minute. I had a meltdown, ran out of the condo, stood in the parking lot, and cried until the car arrived to take us to the airport.

The trip home was equally taxing. I had to carry her bags as well as my own while assisting her by taking her arm. We stopped to split a pizza before going to the gate. While sitting at the gate, I left her alone with the bags while I went to the ladies' room. I explained that she could go next, and I would stay and watch the bags. I'm not one to hang around in a ladies' room, but I admit I made a quick stop at a kiosk to purchase some water and snacks.

When I came back to where she was sitting, she was really angry with me. "Where the hell did you go?" she fumed.

I closed my eyes for a minute to compose myself. "Mom, the bathroom is right there. Look—you can see it from where we're sitting."

"Then why were you gone so long?"

"Can you go by yourself?" I asked.

"Of course," she insisted.

I didn't trust that she could go by herself, so I stood up and watched her walk to the bathroom and stared at the entryway. When she came out, she turned the wrong way and started off down the hall in the opposite direction. I tried calling her, but she didn't hear me. I stood there thinking.

Should I leave the bags and run after her, or should I take them all with me? In a split second, I worried I would lose sight of her, so I ran off after her, leaving the bags behind. I only took my eyes off the bags for a minute, but the whole ordeal really shook me up.

I could see that my mother was growing weary. Between not eating properly, stressing out over closing the condo, and the long walks through the airport, Mom was worn down, and I was fast losing patience.

The plane was delayed, and the passengers were getting restless, so they omitted calling people who needed extra help. Crowds of people hovered over the desk where the woman was trying to check in last-minute travelers, making it difficult to move around. After the people in wheelchairs boarded, I got Mom up, took her arm in mine on one side, put our luggage on the other side, and walked up to the desk.

"Can I take my mother on now? She needs extra help," I asked.

"Does she want a wheelchair?" she responded.

"She won't use a wheelchair."

"Then she can't get on early."

"Really?" I stood there for a moment, perturbed by her bad manners, when suddenly she announced she would be calling more passengers to board in a few minutes. My survival instincts kicked in along with what I thought was great common sense. I took Mom, and instead of sitting back down in our seats, I walked directly to the boarding line. I could feel the people behind me closing in and hear them quietly passing judgment.

"Why is she going to the front of the line?"

I could feel the negativity penetrating me from behind. I felt discomfort in the back of my neck and shoulders and a pit in the core of my stomach. We were almost to the desk, where a young man was waiting to take our boarding passes, when the woman called for the people who paid for early boarding.

"Hey! She said you can't board early," I heard from behind me. "This is for people who paid extra," he added.

He was one of those people who stands in line thirty minutes early, judging other people with his eyes. He's sure he knows everyone's story. He knew about my request because he heard my conversation with the woman at the desk. However, that's all he knew. He didn't know I was dealing with a woman who hallucinated and had Parkinsonian symptoms. He didn't care that she was exhausted, had stiff muscles, but was too proud to use a wheelchair. He didn't know that I almost lost her in the airport twenty minutes earlier. Did he even notice I was carrying her, her luggage, myself, and my luggage? He certainly didn't know that the reason why I made the request was because I didn't want to hold up other passengers. And he didn't know that we *had* early boarding tickets.

I just need a little help, I thought as tears filled my eyes and defeat crushed my soul.

"I did pay extra," I said, trying to turn to address him, but my baggage wouldn't let me.

As we slowly made our way down the Jetway and onto the plane, taking up enough space so no one could pass, I had an unkind sense of satisfaction that the ignorant, ill-mannered man behind me proceeded down the hallway at the same snail's pace as my ailing mother.

When we got off the plane, I could see she was completely exhausted, so I offered again to get her a wheelchair, which she vehemently refused. We made it outside in time to catch the bus, and Tom picked us up at the bus station and drove us home. I helped her up the stairs to her bedroom and brought her something to eat and drink. She managed to get herself undressed and into the bathroom to attempt to take a shower, but she completely ran out of energy and called for me. I went upstairs to find her sitting on the toilet, unable to move. That was the first time I had to shower her. I helped her get into her pajamas, and for the rest of the night, she stayed in her room, unpacking her bags and watching TV, while I stayed downstairs and debriefed Tom on the trip.

Morning came late for Mom as she slowly came down the stairs, emerging as an older and weaker version of herself. Tom and I discussed our concerns about her mobility and decided it was time to move her to our downstairs master bedroom and for us to move upstairs. The boys had all moved out, although Matthew still had some furniture and stuff left in his room. We planned to wait until he got home from sea, giving him a chance to go through his things, but our plans changed a few weeks later when my mother fell in her bathroom.

Standing outside on the deck late one morning, I could hear her yelling for me from her bedroom window. I ran upstairs to find her sitting up against the bathroom door—her inside, me outside. I managed to squeeze the door open enough to get in to check on her, but she told me she couldn't move, so I called for Tom to assist me. It took the two of us to lift her upright, get her to a chair, and calm her down. She insisted she wasn't hurt and refused to go to the hospital. Fearful of another fall, we called a family emergency to recruit enough bodies to make the move that very day. Our bedroom became hers, Matthew's bedroom became ours, and my mother's room became a guest room, all in one afternoon—an immeasurable feat with everyone's busy schedules these days.

The move downstairs brought with it a whole new lifestyle for our family. It also served as a clear reality check for my mother, who eventually gave into the fact that she needed help. Days later, I offered to take over her finances (something I had suggested many times before), but this time she accepted my offer. Tom and I had been supplementing her income for many years, and she'd put my name on her checking account years prior, so it was an easy transition. She had zero savings and a huge credit card debt, so I contacted a financial lawyer to help me negotiate with the credit card companies. I made it perfectly clear that I could only contribute a couple thousand dollars to make the whole mess go away. The lawyer agreed to take my case, but once I paid her fee, she switched gears and told me I needed to come up with a lot more money—money I did not have.

"I should have hired a younger lawyer," I said to Tom.

"Attorney A completely changed the deal?" he surmised from hearing my half of the phone conversation.

"Attorney A didn't even make any sense."

"How old is Attorney A?"

"I think Attorney A has dementia."

"How drastic is the change?"

"It's a deal-breaker."

"All that time, energy, and money for nothing?"

"Yep. I'm going to get some of the retainer back, and I guess I'll have to find a plan B."

So we were back to square one with the finances. I paid a small portion to the credit cards and full payments to the two home equity loans, HOA, and utilities. I continued to make phone calls to banks seeking advice, help, or relief, but the status never changed. I agonized over how my mother managed her finances with so little coming in and so many bills, but I found comfort in knowing she was happy to have relinquished that torture.

~

That summer, I started the heavy task of getting my mother Medicaid, which required taking her to the social security office to change her address from Florida to our address, going to the hospital office to start the process and have her interviewed, changing her primary care doctor, making endless phone calls, filling out endless forms, and submitting endless paperwork like bank statements, etc. In order to qualify, the individual has to have a very low income and no worldly possessions. Mom was close, but her social security was a smidge over, so she had to qualify for a frail elder waiver, which is administered by a nurse provided by elder services—another phone call and appointment.

Elder services is a great resource for answering questions and steering you in the right direction for your particular needs. And the people are kind beyond words. They told me about a program called Caregiver Homes, which assists with in-home caregiving. They pay a daily stipend determined by the level of care and state adult foster care regulations, and provide a caseworker and a nurse who make monthly visits to your home. They are an enormous help, offer excellent support, and provide great resources. It's well worth the effort to research qualification.

While I was looking for help with long-term home care, my mother was insisting she was well enough to go to Florida. Although my heart was heavy for her loss of independence, my empathy was waning because she made it so difficult for me.

"Peggy, where's my driver's license?" she yelled from the other side of the house.

"I don't know. Check your wallet," I yelled back.

"I *did!*"

"Why would I have your license?"

"Did you take it?"

"*No.*"

I went in to her room and looked in the usual places but did not find it. Two days later, she walked into the kitchen with her license in hand.

"Look—I found my license," she hissed.

"Where?" I asked.

"It was in with your rubble." (Of course, it wasn't her doing.)

"That's why you can't go to Florida—because you can't find your license!" I said in a huff.

"Wouldn't you like that!" she huffed right back.

Days later, she brought it up again. "I need to go back to Florida," she said.

"You really can't stay there alone," I replied.

"I'll have to find someone who will take me."

"That's a good idea. What about your other children?"

Silence. There was always silence when I suggested one of her other children helping with her care in any way, shape, or form.

"If I take you to Florida, would you be willing to get in a wheelchair at the airport?" I asked. I actually considered taking her for a month or so.

"Absolutely not," she replied, which only served to ease my pain. If she wouldn't even consider making my life easier, why would I consider putting myself through hell to take her to Florida? She'd have better luck asking one of my brothers to take her. If I only had sisters!

My go-to phrase—"if I only had sisters"—was getting old and getting me nowhere, so I created my own group of support sisters. They became my lifeline to sanity on a regular basis. They filled my soul, warmed my heart, and saved me from despair. They were the ones who took time out of their busy schedules on a regular basis to make mine and my mother's lives that much easier. I texted my "sister" Gigi.

I'm about to pop my cork. You busy?

I'm free. Pour yourself a glass of wine and call me.

I would proceed to vomit emotions for a good hour. It was wonderfully satisfying to purge the anger and frustration I was internalizing.

When I had a medical question, I called my "sister" Lynne. If she didn't have an answer, she would find one, and get right back to me with her insightful information. She was also continually concerned about my well-being as a caretaker, as she was in the same boat with her dad. She knew how difficult it was performing that role, so we would commiserate often.

I called my "sister" Diane to take care of my mother when I needed to be away from home. My mother needed help getting dressed, and that was one task Tom wasn't comfortable tending to, but Diane said she was happy to help. She went above and beyond, playing dress-up, makeup, sharing her homemade desserts over coffee, taking her for a long drive through the back roads of New England, or taking her out to lunch. My mother loved her time with her—and Tom and I loved the break. Diane always left my mother with a stockpile of cakes and cookies, leaving her love behind to enjoy for days on end.

My friend Angela was there to do anything I asked—anytime. She was my perfect impromptu "sister."

"I've got to get out of here—now," was all she needed to hear, and within the hour, she would pick me up and take me away. No questions asked. Angela also had firsthand knowledge of my mother's paranoia and behavior, so she understood the situation better than most. And, she's a really good person—the kind with a true, pure heart. She'll listen all day long with interest and concern, yet you'll never hear one negative word in response. She kept me grounded and kept me from going over to the dark side.

If I had a dementia question, I called my "sister" Kim. She works full time and has two small children, one with autism. But she always found the time to check in on me. She was going through a similar situation with her aunt, so she was helpful with what behaviors to look for and how to resolve problems that arose.

My vision of this special group of people in my life was analogous to her son's communication board. The board had laminated pieces with various pictures on one side and Velcro on the other, enabling him to take them on or off the board to communicate his needs. My support system was on an imaginary communication board in my heart, and I could reach out to any of my "sisters" for a particular need.

TEN

One Step Down, One Level Up

THE AIR CONDITIONER was chugging away in the window on a hot August night in 2013 when a bad feeling sat me up straight in bed. I had been meaning to hook up a baby monitor to Mom's room, but I honestly didn't think we were at that point. Besides, nap? Deep sleep? It didn't matter; I always woke up the minute one of my children or grandchildren made a peep. Some people at the support group I had attended earlier that month told me I was in denial, and as it turned out, they were right. We *were* at that point.

"Tom, wake up. Do you hear something?" I whispered.

He raised his head, listened for a moment, and then jumped out of bed. "It's your mother!" he yelled.

We both flew downstairs to find her lying on the floor, on her stomach, beside her bed.

"Oh my God, Mom, are you OK?" I cried.

"I've been lying here for hours," she said furiously.

"I'm so sorry. I didn't hear you."

"I called you two thousand times."

Tom asked her a list of questions and had her move certain body parts to evaluate her before we picked her up and sat her on the chair.

"I'm going to call 911," I said.

"No!" she yelled.

"I'm afraid you're hurt."

"I'm fine. I don't want to go to the hospital."

We sat with her for a couple of hours to calm her down and make sure she was all right. She seemed to be fine, so we helped her back to bed. Tom went back to bed upstairs while I slept on the couch on the other side of her bedroom wall.

The following morning Mom said she was fine but a little sore, and the day marched on as usual. She was wandering around demonstrating her typical behavior, but when she sat down to watch the television around two o'clock in the afternoon, she fell asleep in her chair. Mom never took a nap, never closed her eyes while sitting in a chair, not for a minute—not ever. She went to lie down in her bed around three o'clock, refused to get up for dinner, and stayed there until morning. Concerned, I reached out to my support system, specifically the ones with medical knowledge. They each told me she was probably just tired from the fall, that I should watch her and take her to the doctor in the morning.

Easier said than done, I learned.

"Hello, I'd like to make an appointment for my mother," I said to the woman who answered the phone at her doctor's office.

"I'm sorry, but we don't have anything available," she replied.

"I really think she should be seen. She fell around three a.m. the night before last and was exceedingly lethargic all day yesterday."

"I'm sorry, but we don't have anything open for today. You could take her to the walk-in clinic."

"That's a half hour away, and I don't know how long we'll have to sit there to be seen. She's elderly. I think it would be cruel to make her sit in a waiting room for hours when she's not feeling well."

"I'm sorry, but there's nothing I can do for her today."

"I guess I'll just have to take her to the ER." I was hoping she would find some sympathy.

"You're certainly welcome to do that, but it will cost a lot more in co-payments than taking her to the walk-in clinic."

The fact that Mom didn't make even the slightest bit of fuss about seeing the doctor worried me. I took her to the ER.

Having been through countless weekend stitches with the boys, hours of visiting friends, and a few family emergencies, I was well aware of how the local ER functioned. A quick check-in was followed by a visit with the triage nurse, who took information and vitals. From there you were instructed to take a seat in the waiting room and wait anywhere between fifteen minutes and four hours. The ultimate goal was to get through the massive doors, which required a special code or an employee swipe, where you would be checked in by a nurse and treated by a doctor. On this visit, the procedure was altered. We weren't sent back to the waiting room—we went straight through the massive doors.

"Get her on a gurney; she's in a-fib!" cried the triage nurse. A-fib, or atrial fibrillation, is a condition that causes rapid and irregular beating of the heart—in Mom's case, her heart rate was very fast, and her blood pressure was very low.

"You're kidding me," I squealed.

"If she's not treated immediately, she's in danger of having a stroke," said the ER nurse, breaking the hospital's speed limit with the gurney. "Once her heart rate is under control, we'll treat her for the fall."

"Would you also test her for a urinary tract infection?" I asked. For Mom, as with the elderly population in general, it wasn't just the falls that caused her harm, it was the underlying reason for the falls.

Hours later, with her heart under control, they took her for some images to see if she had broken anything when she fell. She had not. Then they did an ultrasound on her belly and found gallstones and an inflamed bladder. Soon thereafter the urinalysis came back positive for a UTI. Nine hours later they admitted her. We hadn't had an official LBD diagnosis, as we were two months away from the neurologist appointment, but I was positive she had the disease. Painstakingly and with Mom out of earshot, I told every doctor, aide, and nurse who came in contact with her that she had LBD. She would not have approved of sharing such information and would have firmly denied it.

I carefully explained to each medical professional that people with LBD can't take certain drugs. Although I was not equipped with the specific information, I assumed the hospital was. Not surprisingly, none of them had ever heard of Lewy body dementia, let alone had any knowledge of the particulars around treating it. Exhausted, hungry, and nauseated (and against my better judgment), I left my mother in the ER while she waited for a bed on the seventh floor of the hospital—at least another two hours, I was told. I pleaded with the ER nurse to pass along the information about LBD, how patients can't take just any drug, and please tell the nurses on the seventh floor. I should have listened to my instinct when it told me to go up to the seventh floor and tell the people on duty, but instead, I went home and hooked up the baby monitor.

In her hospital room the following morning, I found Mom sitting in a chair with both her hands curled into fists, thumbs together, fists touching each other. Her arms were resting on her stomach as she shook her fists up and down, and her body was rocking back and forth as she stared blankly at the wall. She was completely whacked out, and it wasn't long before I was too. I was panic-stricken! I knew that the use of psychotropic drugs had caused permanent damage to the brain with some LBD patients. I burst into tears.

"Oh Mama…Mama…Mama…what did they do to you?" I screamed.

She couldn't speak; she just moaned. I walked around the room for a few minutes trying to process the situation; then I bent down to get closer to her.

"Oh, Mama, what happened?"

She started to speak, but it sounded like she had a pound of cotton in her mouth. I was frozen helpless, staring at her completely traumatized.

"…kill myself," were the only tongueless words I understood.

"Would you please get her nurse?" I cried to the young aide in the room.

I called Tom but could barely speak through my sobbing. He wasn't able to get to the hospital immediately, so he called John and Matthew to see if either was available to rescue me. Soon thereafter Nurse North came in and told me they gave her Ativan in the middle of the night because she was trying to get up to go to the bathroom. Just a small dose of

Ativan caused my mother to "snow"—a term used for patients who have a really bad reaction to a drug. Nurse North told me she had been like that since around three o'clock in the morning.

"She has Lewy body disease," I fumed.

"I know," replied Nurse North.

"I told everyone in the ER."

She released a sympathetic sigh and stared.

"You have to be careful about what kind of drugs you give her," I pleaded.

"I'll tell the doctor you would like to speak with her," Nurse North said in a soft tone.

I paced, cried, and stared at my mother. The young aide was trying to comfort me while unsuccessfully trying to keep her assigned patient in her bed. Mom's roommate had been given the maximum amount of medication allowed to keep her quiet, in bed, and safe from wandering. One woman who wouldn't go down with a megadose, and one woman who was completely whacked out on the minimum dose, side by side in the same room, accompanied by a sweet little aide and a hysterical daughter.

"Can you get the patient advocate?" I asked the aide.

"I don't know what that is," she replied.

"Whoever is on duty to protect the rights of the patients."

"Oh, we have caseworkers. Every patient has one."

"Never mind, my boys are coming."

"That's good," she said.

"I'm sure I'll see the caseworker at some point."

I believe that John and Matthew were just as freaked out as I was when they first saw their grandmother in that condition, but they soon realized that two freaked-out grandchildren on top of a freaked-out daughter would not help the situation. They walked me out of the room, down the hall, and out of the sight of any doctors, nurses, visitors, or patients, and then calmed me down.

"Mom, obviously I see why you're upset, but there's nothing you can do about it right now, so—" said John.

I didn't hear or don't remember the rest of his advice, but the boys were successful at reassuring me things would be all right enough that I could manage the situation. The path I was on wasn't helping anything or anyone. I went back to the room with much more composure.

While I was there watching over Mom, I could see a young woman going in and out of the nurses' station as she and the others looked at me in a peculiar manner. I suspected she was the doctor I had been waiting hours to see, but I wasn't impressed with *any* doctors when it came to how to deal with LBD, so I was in no hurry to have another fruitless conversation with her. I was scared and angry. I would avoid me too!

"Hello, I'm Doctor Bold. You wanted to see me?" she announced as she made her entrance. She had plenty of time to compose herself and plan her strategy.

"I told *everyone* I spoke to yesterday that she has Lewy body disease. Every person!" I said, my voice raised.

"And?" she said defensively.

"You can't use the same protocol with people who have this disease."

"Giving her Ativan was the right thing to do."

"No, it wasn't. How can you even say that? Look at her."

"Francesca, how are you feeling?" Doctor Bold asked, but Mom didn't even look at her.

"She can't speak," I wailed.

"Look, that's what we do when people get agitated. We gave her the smallest amount of Ativan possible just to calm her down so she wouldn't try to get out of her bed and hurt herself."

"She gets agitated at home too, but we turn on the television or take her for a walk or sit with her for a minute. We don't drug her up so she can't even function."

"Look, it was the right thing to do, and I would do it again. Not with Ativan, but with a different drug." Why wouldn't anyone listen to me? Was it was because she was elderly? When Tom was in the hospital, everyone was very nice. His doctors not only listened to me, they welcomed my input and made adjustments accordingly.

No, you won't. You will not be giving my mother any more drugs, I thought. I requested a private room and told the nurse I would be spending the night by her bedside.

For the next twenty hours, I was my mother's human straitjacket. The hospital didn't have a cot for me, so they provided me with a chair that reclined, which was where I spent the night. When she reached her arms out to the ceiling and waved them around, I pulled them back by her side. When she rolled up the blanket and pulled it up to her waist, I straightened it out and covered her legs and feet. When she wasn't moaning, she was screaming about water, so I stroked her forehead and whispered gently in her ear. She was on a plane, and a train, in a car, and back on the plane again. She screamed for my one-year-old granddaughter to come to her. "Patty, get out of the water."

"Matthew, get her."

"Oh, *no*! Someone get that baby, please."

"Help!"

She moaned, screamed, whimpered, flung her arms, and pulled at her blankets all through the night, until around four o'clock, when she recognized my voice and called me by name. Shortly after that, Nurse Night came in, and my mother picked up her head to see her. "Oh, look at you. Don't you look nice," Mom said.

"Well, you look good yourself," Nurse Night said.

"You must be going out."

"Not yet, but pretty soon," Nurse Night replied.

"Listen, you girls drink like ladies now."

"Oh, we will."

"I use the Sign of the Cross. I find that helps. But then again, I have my own set of rules. You do what's best for you."

"I see she's coming around." Nurse Night smiled.

"Yes, she may not be making any sense, but at least she's forming sentences," I replied.

"I need to use the bathroom," said Mom.

"I'll get you a bedpan. We don't want you moving yet," explained Nurse Night.

"OK, boys, go away. Don't look because it may not look like yours," Mom said.

I knew she was talking to invisible boys, but at that point, I didn't care. I was extremely grateful that she was speaking in sentences. For the next couple of hours, she went from peaceful sleep to short bouts of restless sleep and back to peaceful sleep. When she was awake, she spoke with her nurse and aide with her normal pleasant personality.

"I see what you mean. She is very sweet," Nurse Night said.

"I get it. When my mother has a UTI, she is nastier than a disturbed bear! But that's not her normal personality. Really!" I said.

"I can see that."

"If I go home for a little bit, will you please not sedate her?"

"I won't, and I'll speak with the nurse relieving me. I understand."

"I won't be long, but please call me if you need me. I'll come right back."

"OK, just leave your cell phone number on the whiteboard."

"Done!"

Mom had snowed on Ativan for thirty hours.

At five o'clock that morning, I went home and Tom went to the hospital, bringing her coffee and a muffin. She ate while they chatted together. She made sense and was able to hold a conversation, so he took her for a walk down the hallway and back to her room. Meanwhile, I slept for three hours. Tom had a scheduled trip to London that day and needed to leave for the airport around noon, but I wasn't totally comfortable leaving Mom alone, so I went back to the hospital around ten o'clock to relieve him. I spent a couple of hours with her and could see she was feeling better and behaving more like her normal self. I, on the other hand, was completely drained. I could easily pull an all-nighter in my twenties and even in my thirties, but doing so in my midfifties took a toll on my body as well as my brain. "Mom, I'm going to go home for the rest of the day," I insisted.

"I don't want you to go," she pleaded.

"I know."

"Don't go yet."

"You're fine. I've been here all night, and I really need to get some sleep."

"But I really want you to stay and visit with me."

"Mom, may I remind you that the two times I was in the hospital, you didn't come to visit me once?"

"Oh, that's different—you have Tom."

"Yes, and I also have three brothers, but you don't see them here!"

I was annoyed.

"Well, that's OK," Mom said. "I don't expect them to come and visit me."

I let out a deep sigh.

From that point on, she didn't want me to leave her side—ever. And if I did have to leave, she wanted to come with me. I had to find clever tactics to leave without her knowing, or she would throw a fit. For the first time, I used an approach that would become practice for the remainder of our time together.

"I'll be right back," I said and slipped out the door.

$\sim$

Mom stayed in the hospital for five days and left with orders to follow up with a cardiologist, her primary care doctor, and the hospital for another kidney scan. From the hospital, she had orders to go to a nursing home for rehabilitation. I had a choice to send her to a new state-of-the-art facility about twenty minutes from my home or an older one right down the street; I chose the latter. I was thrilled to have her so close, as it enabled me to run home between visits to bring her food or anything she requested from home. The people at the local facility were extremely kind and tremendously pleasing. She settled in quite nicely and was particularly fond of the young female aides.

One of the aides came in to help her to the bathroom and accidently knocked the phone off the table. It hit the ground with a loud bang and flustered the young girl. "Oh my goodness; I'm so sorry!" she exclaimed.

My mother, who had developed a difficult time maneuvering a phone, was unfazed. "That's OK, maybe you'll knock some sense into it," she joked.

Days later during a visit, I was keeping myself busy crocheting, while she was wandering around her room. Someone came in with a card for her. She painstakingly opened it up, and we heard a loud scream—then: "I feel good, dadadadadadada…I knew that I would!"

It was one of those cards that when opened would play a song. This one in particular was James Brown's "I Feel Good." The scream caught us off guard, and we both quickly stared at each other in shock until the song started playing—then we burst into laughter. She played it again, and we laughed some more.

"I think I just lost an inch off my waist," she giggled.

I decided that this was Lewy-speak for "I think I just came within an inch of my life."

Considering she was safe, taken care of, and relatively happy at the nursing home, I was able to join Tom on a business trip to the Napa Valley in California. Tom had invited me on many business trips throughout our married life together, but I almost always declined the invitation, citing the boys, work, and the house. Now that the boys were all grown up and I was out of work, I should have been able to say yes to all his invitations, but again I found myself declining most of them because I had to care for my mother. This time I jumped at the chance to get away. I enjoyed a wonderful, warm, relaxing trip to California that entailed a guided tour from a Napa native; exploration of places in a winery that most people don't have the privilege of seeing; a picnic on a private piece of land surrounded by water, geese, and natural beauty; late-night drinks and conversations with friends rarely seen; warm weather; and free time to read, think, and meditate, as well as precious quiet time alone with Tom.

Then it was Mom's turn. We reentered reality and brought Mom back home the day after we returned from our trip. She had been away for a month and was thrilled to resume life as she remembered it. A visiting nurse, an occupational therapist, and a physical therapist each came twice a week to help her transition to normalcy, and a woman came to shower her twice a week.

I took over administering her medications. She really didn't want to give up yet another bit of independence, but I was worried about her forgetting to take them, so I transitioned into taking over the job. I also had to take her blood pressure every morning, record it, and, depending on the reading, hold back a pill or two. Taking over the job entirely was the sensible thing to do.

After that hospital and rehab stay, my mother's hallucinations had become so much a part of her normalcy that she freely shared them with others. The Parkinsonian symptoms were progressing as well. Her muscles were getting stiff, and she had a very difficult time reversing direction. When she got up from her chair, she went straight ahead into the kitchen through one entryway, through the kitchen, and out the other entryway, completing a loop through the entire house before going into her bedroom—which was just steps behind her if she could just turn around. She spent a minute or two in her bedroom before returning to sit in her chair for a bit.

"Where are you going, Francesca?" Tom asked, knowing full well what her motives were.

"I have to see what's going on in there," she said.

She came back to her chair for a few minutes and then got up and slowly took the long route back to her bedroom.

"Where are you going now, Francesca?"

"I'm going to see who's in my room now. It was mobbed in there last night!"

Tom got up to walk into the bedroom with her.

"I can see the TV on," she announced.

"No, Francesca, the TV's not on. Did you have it on when you went to bed last night?"

"No, but the kids turned it on in the middle of the night."

"When the kids turn it on in the middle of the night, do they watch the cartoon channel or Fox News?"

No reply—she didn't get the joke.

"All right, I'll chase the kids out," he said.

Poor Mom was as frustrated as one could possibly be with all the people she hallucinated, but while the kids may have been a little annoying, the men really angered her. Tom and I tried everything we could think of to get rid of the men, but they kept coming back.

"What does this man look like?" I queried.

"What do you mean?" she yelled. "You walked right by him!"

"All right," Tom yelled in his best authoritative voice. "That's it. Everybody out!" This scene, or something similar to it, played out hundreds of times. We were never really sure if our efforts worked or if she just gave up and dealt with her situation as best she could. At that time, I thought our efforts worked (at least to some extent), but in hindsight, I think they probably didn't. The men always came back. No doubt the men were a problem, and soon the remedy would become an even bigger problem—for me.

ELEVEN

To Med or Not to Med... That Is the Question

MOM'S THERAPY CONTINUED for six weeks, and before I knew it the visiting nurse, the occupational therapist, the physical therapist, and the shower angel all stopped coming, leaving me to fend for myself. The therapists' goals were to get her back to where she was before the fall, but they could only work their magic so far. Our long-awaited neurologist appointment was just a few weeks away, giving me hope for help, although Mom made it quite clear that she didn't need help, hope, or a neurologist. Anticipating a battle, I asked Tom to take the afternoon off from work and come along with me for support. I was pleasantly surprised when she got into the car with no complaining, but I later learned she thought she was going to the periodontist. She loved seeing any doctor who treated her teeth. Her brain? Not so much.

When she realized we'd arrived at a medical facility, she became frightened, angry, and stubborn. When she refused to get out of the car, we had to coax and then coerce her into the building. She sat in the waiting area with Tom while I spoke with the woman at the desk. I told her that Mom was reticent about seeing the doctor and asked how long the wait would be. She informed me that Dr. Wonderful Neurologist prided himself on being right on time and gave me a questionnaire for Mom to complete. Most of the questions dealt with emotional well-being. I read the questions out loud and circled her responses. She gave positive responses to every question. She continued to believe that denying the disease would make Lewy turn around and go away. Happy little bubble.

Five minutes before her appointment, a young woman came out to the waiting room and introduced herself as a physical therapist and assistant. She took Mom for a walk, and once she was comfortable with her stability, she asked her to walk down the hallway alone so she could observe her movements, making notes about her gait and the absence of any swing in her arms. She then escorted Mom and me to a room and began to ask questions. I assisted Mom with her answers by rephrasing them to what she was really trying to say. She began to lose the ability to find appropriate wording, so she substituted them with something she thought would work. During this visit, Mom used the word *canteen* when she meant to say *café* and *time bomb* when she was referring to her electric blanket. I learned to listen very carefully and think outside the box to make sense of what she was trying to explain. Sometimes it was easy. Other times, I needed to take a long pause to piece the thought together in my brain before passing it along to her recipient. I became her interpreter.

The doctor was kind and gentle with Mom, and she was determined to be as normal as the doctor. He asked her to take off her sneakers, and she whipped them off faster than a little kid at the beach. I stared in amazement. It would take her at least fifteen minutes to take them off at home. He examined her body, took her vitals, and looked up the CT scan of her brain in her online records. He then asked her a number of questions about her hallucinations. She proceeded to tell him about the cat that peed everywhere, the birds, the bugs, the babies, the women who hated her, some with no legs, and the men who often climbed into her bed and frightened her. His kind and understanding responses led Mom to believe she finally found someone who accepted her hallucinations as real. She was so comfortable with his sincere interest that she went into greater detail about the men in particular.

"They're about forty years old and have huge coats with lots of feathers," she said. "They have magic keys because they don't need doors to get into the house."

She was quite pleased that she'd finally found someone who believed her.

"OK, would you please write your name on a piece of paper?" he asked.

Her penmanship was very small and went up on a slant. He looked at the paper, pushed his chair back, and proceeded to say the words that my mother absolutely did not want to hear. "Well, Francesca, you should give your daughter a lot of credit. She was right all along. You have Lewy body disease."

She was furious! "Let's go, Peggy. This doctor is a quack!" Mom raged.

She looked at the assistant who was sitting quietly in the corner taking notes.

"You believe me, don't you?" she said to the young woman.

"I believe you see what you see," she replied.

My mother stared at her, waiting for her to defy her daughter and the doctor.

"But I agree with the doctor," she added.

"I'm not going to stop until I find someone who does believe me," Mom insisted. "I'll just have to find a reporter who's willing to investigate this."

"I do believe you see these things, but they're not real," the doctor said.

"Oh, yes, they *are* real," she said.

"Francesca, do you dream at night when you sleep?" he asked calmly.

She was indignant at this point and was now down to one-word answers. "Yes."

"Well, it's like you're dreaming, only with your eyes open."

"It is not!"

Realizing that she was incapable of reasoning, he then took a more clinical approach. "Francesca, your reality is not consistent with other people's reality because of changes in your brain structure and brain chemistry. I can prescribe you a drug that would make the men go away."

"Drugs won't make them go away. It's not in my mind. They're real!"

"Some people don't mind their hallucinations. Some even find comfort in them. Like the babies in their beds. They keep them company."

She sat in silence with her arms crossed and stared out the window.

"Our society considers you to be free to live in your own reality as long as you don't harm yourself or others. There's one particular case where a man saw bees coming at him and would run out of the house into the middle of the street to get away from them. In this case, we had to intervene with treatment," he continued.

She wouldn't even look at him, so he directed his explanation toward me.

"I'd like to see you again. Would you come back for another appointment in three months?"

"No!"

"OK, how about four months? Would you consider that?"

She was silent; he took that as a yes.

We went out to the waiting room, where I told Tom to take her to the car while I made another appointment for her. I asked if I could speak with the assistant who was in the room with us.

"Can you tell me about the medication?" I asked.

"We use Quetiapine, and they would start with a very low dose, but we can't administer it without her consent."

"I understand. I'd like to do some research on it, just in case."

"If you think your mother is in distress and really needs the medication, then give us a call, and we'll take it from there."

When we got into the car, I received the all-too-familiar lecture, complete with the finger in my face. "I will not go back to that quack, and that's all there is to it!" she said.

"OK, Mom," I replied.

"I don't understand why you don't believe me."

"I know, Mom."

"I guess I'm just going to have to find someone who will."

"OK."

"I *will* find someone who believes me."

"Mom, how about we stop for an early dinner and nice glass of wine?"

She was silent; I took that as a yes.

TWELVE

———— ∿ ————

*You don't even realize how much you accomplish
in a day.*

—Francesca Jean

After that visit, Tom became more involved with my mother's daily care. It was a harsh reality check for him, and it became painfully clear that this was going to be our way of life for a while. He did as much as he could to give me little breaks by taking her for her daily walk around the block or for a ride in the car. It was also clear that she couldn't go back to Florida, so we would have to make some relationship adjustments. We absolutely loved having her with us, but we also enjoyed our alone time while she was away. Even our few moments alone were consumed with talk of my mother and her issues. As for my mother, I hoped she would find a way to enjoy fall in New England. I know, asking a snowbird to "enjoy" winter in New England is a stretch, but for now, I could only tackle one season at a time.

While most of my mother's hallucinations were annoying but harmless (she threw her backpack away because the cat peed in it or she would chase the invisible cat around the house), the men were a whole different story.

"He won't even take me on a date, but he thinks he can sleep with me!" she said.

"That's crazy."

"Why won't they just leave me alone?"

"I don't know," I lied.

At times, she got so upset that I would have to lie down in bed with her, taking up the space that the man occupied. When she fell asleep, I would sneak out to my own bed. One evening, she actually threw a big, heavy upholstered antique chair across the room because he was sitting on it and wouldn't leave at her request. I don't know how she found the strength to pick it up, let alone throw it. But our attempts to get rid of the men weren't working. The men were upsetting her to the point where it was affecting her daily well-being. I began to think she needed more help.

I also began to think maybe it was time for that medication.

It was time to learn more about that drug. After looking through websites, I decided I needed a more personal touch, so I reached out to two cousins—Farah, a physician's assistant, and Ellen, a pharmacist. Ellen was confident that the drug would be safe for my mother. Farah, on the other hand, had a completely different point of view. Her biggest concern was the simple fact that my mother didn't want to take the drug. Anyone in the medical field will honor the patient's wishes over the caregiver's needs—*unless* the patient is causing harm to herself or others. Farah is also a deeply spiritual woman who believed that my mother's intuition was weighing in on her adamantly refusing to take medications. Some people may call it an instinct, while others may say she was just being stubborn. Farah was also concerned about the side effects. After giving me their best opinions and facts, they each told me they would support me with whatever I decided to do. But before I would be able to do anything, I had to evaluate and be sure my mother was in enough distress to even intervene. I really didn't want to medicate her, but my heart broke for her every day after four o'clock when she would become so upset with the men. And at this point, all our efforts to get them out of her room were definitely not working. So the conversation started with the two little people on each of my shoulders:

She's scared.

But she's alert—those pills may make her drowsy.

It breaks my heart when she screams at the men to get out of her bed.

So, your children did the same thing when they were little; you didn't medicate them.

But that's different. Children have developing brains and imaginations—she has hallucinations and a disease.

She doesn't want it.

But she needs it.

Who's going to monitor her...you? How will you give it to her? You can't just wing it. You need a plan.

I'll sneak it in some applesauce.

You think you can sneak it to her every day? She doesn't want it!

But she's so *scared*. Really scared—*every* night!

And down the rabbit hole I went! I entered a state of chaos, confusion, and the unknown. So I sat on the couch for a few days, not dealing. Like a child's top, my head was spinning out of control. My brain simply shut down. "This is so hard," I said over and over.

Over the next few weeks, I researched websites, made phone calls, and texted Farah. I'm not sure I was very productive, but then again, I'm not sure anyone is very productive while down in the rabbit hole. A few weeks later, I saw Ellen and Farah at a family Christmas party. They each made a point to see how I was doing and chat with me for a bit, but all I could do was cry.

I can't hear you. I can't see you. I'm down here in a hole, and my brain's not working! I thought.

"I'm so sorry if my comments are making your decision more difficult," said Farah.

I grabbed a tissue from my purse.

"Peggy, I was giving advice from a clinical point of view. A medical professional will always try to honor the patient's wishes, but many people don't get the kind of care and support that you're giving your mother," she added.

"It's just so hard, Farah," I said.

"I know. You're coming from a wonderful place of love. You should do what you think is best. We'll all totally support your decision."

The lump in my throat wouldn't let me speak, so I responded with a hug.

Shortly after that party, my mother had an appointment with her primary care physician, so I just hung out in my hole, hoping that appointment would solve all our problems. Doctor Primary Care Number Three was kind and gentle. She read the report from the neurologist and began to have a discussion with my mother about the suggested medication.

"I hate pills," Mom said.

"OK," replied the doctor.

"I hate what they do to me!"

"OK."

And that was that; Doctor Primary Care Number Three would have to honor her wishes. She explained to my mother that she could not take her off all her medication, as she was at risk of having a heart attack or stroke without them, but we would abstain from prescribing any new medications.

"As long as you don't hurt yourself," Doctor Primary Care Number Three said as we got up to leave.

"Hang in there," she whispered to me as we walked out the door.

As we left the office, I felt a great sense of relief. I really didn't want to medicate her. But I thought it was cruel not to intervene somehow, because our current course of action wasn't working, and she was living with agonizing fear.

I told Farah about the appointment. "That's good news," she said.

"At least it takes the heart-wrenching decision process away from me for now," I replied.

"In the meantime, Peg, be strong. Empower yourself with all the information that you get from all your resources, and when the time comes that you need to make another decision, let it be yours."

"Good advice."

"Your mother is giving you an incredible opportunity to know who you are and to be strong, on a spiritual level."

That night, I had a vivid dream. I was in the doctor's office with someone going through treatment. I watched helplessly as they accepted the pain they were experiencing in an effort to get better. Then it was my turn. I was the one on the table being prepped for—what? I didn't know what was wrong with me.

"Where does it hurt? Where's your pain?" a voice asked.

"Well...nowhere," I answered. "I'm not sick. So why are you treating me?"

I woke up and immediately thought of Farah and Mother Mary. I took it as a sign that I'd made the right decision—or that the right decision was made for me. I jumped out of bed and grabbed my journal, and as I started to write, I could feel myself calming down. I mentally thanked Farah for pulling me out of that particular rabbit hole. I thought about Farah's words quite a bit after that: "Empower yourself. Let the decision be yours!"

This ordeal around medication was draining. I found myself reflecting on those words often in order to get through the day in one piece. So I decided to give myself the gift of "one day at a time." My head was focused on my mother's physical care, while my heart was breaking into little pieces. As much as I tried to stay positive, look at all the blessings, and enjoy the time with my sweet mother, every day was exhausting— physically and emotionally. Instead of fixating on the big picture, I made my best effort to get through each day with as little bruising as possible—for all of us. The "one-day-at-a-time" approach, along with Farah's advice, gave me a sense of calm and enabled me to discuss my mother's condition in a sensible tone—as opposed to the angry, loud, frustrated, and fearful tone I had been using previously.

That is, until the next crisis came around the corner.

∽

I was completely mesmerized by the Lewy brain. Every morning, we were greeted with a new set of issues, along with the constant array of mischief that happened in my mother's room throughout the evening while she slept. The cats, birds, bugs, babies, women, and men, among others, played a daily role in our lives. The cat was a problem because it peed all over the place. The cat was also known to crawl into her bed and hide down by her feet. Many nights, I would have to pull the blankets almost completely off the bed to reveal the absence of a cat. Sometimes it worked; sometimes she went to bed unhappy with my lack of productivity. The cat would also get into the toothpaste and eat it. One morning, I went in her bathroom and found her toothbrush, toothpaste, and toothbrush holder in the trash. I learned that I had to go in her bathroom after she went to sleep and clean up her mess, because when she got up in the morning, her nighttime mess became the cat's annoying play.

The birds were a problem because from the time she was a very young girl, she had been told they were bad luck. She said they gave her "the willies." All birds. She could barely eat chicken. But even people who like birds don't like them in their beds. The birds pooped everywhere and were particularly fond of leaving their mess in her closet. Their shedding feathers annoyed her persistently.

The bugs were everywhere. Most of the bugs were black, but the bugs on her bed were pink and green. I'm sure they transformed from her bedding. When I changed her bed sheets, I alternated between two sets, one pink and the other blue. But the electric blanket that warmed her bed every night was 1960s lime green. We plugged it in thirty minutes before bedtime and unplugged it before she went to sleep. She finally had enough of the pink and green bugs on the bed, and because I failed to get rid of them, she decided to take matters into her own hands. One day I could smell something awful coming from her room and went in to find her spraying everything with bug killer. Everything—her body, her bed, her clothes, the closet, the walls—nothing was safe from the pesticide. My heart sank with the thoughts of her mind being so off that she would find relief by poisoning herself, so I convinced her that room spray would work better and gave her a can. Thank goodness she believed me (and as a bonus, her room always smelled lovely).

The babies were troublesome. Not because they bothered her but because they weren't with their rightful owners. Plus she was afraid she would roll over onto them or the men in the bed would harm them. When she was in Florida, she would plead with me to call the people who were dropping their kids off at her condo. She described the vehicle that delivered them. It was a white van that could carry about ten children.

I flashed back to a summer many years ago when we were young. My mother was working full time, so when school ended, my brothers and I had to go to daycare for two weeks because she couldn't find a sitter for that time frame. The facility came equipped with its very own white van that picked us up in the morning. As a child born into a huge Italian family in the late fifties, I had never been to daycare. At any given moment, I had at least fifteen aunts and uncles and thirty-some-odd cousins all within walking distance and all watching over one another. Any time one of us called out "Mom," there would be five women available to tend to our needs. Grandma was always home, cooking or tending her garden. Quite often, she had grandchildren running around her yard among her flowers and vegetables. I wondered if my mother had gone back to that time in her mind and created the same scenario as a means to explain all the children running around her home.

The issues with the women varied. Young girls were fine, although they often had hidden messages that only she understood.

"Look at her; she's wearing my scarves!" she said.

I looked at where she was referring to and saw a small hat rack, about four feet high, with five scarves on it.

"That's a hat rack with your scarves on it," I said, ever trying to get her to snap out of it.

"Oh, I know. But look at her, she's trying on my scarves."

I sighed and looked at her sympathetically.

"And look at the one on the chair over there. She has no legs."

"No legs, Mom?"

"She must work for a medical company. She's probably documenting everything I do."

While the young girls were entertaining and harmless, the older women really intimidated her. They would pass judgment on by her making funny faces at her. Sometimes the faces were angry, other times disapproving.

None of these characters made any noise, not a meow, peep, hello, or hey you; they communicated to her with their facial expressions.

The men continued to be a major problem. The day men wore huge coats made of feathers, and the sight frightened her. She could describe them perfectly and couldn't understand why they didn't unnerve the rest of the world. But most upsetting of all were the evening men. They were in her bed every night. Sometimes they were naked. Sometimes they were playing with themselves.

"Who do they think they are?" she said.

"Where is he right now?"

She gave me a disapproving look. She was cognizant enough to realize that by asking the question, I was expressing that I didn't see them.

"Where is he?" I asked again.

"In the chair right there!"

"Am I sitting on him?" I asked as I jumped on the chair, pleased with myself.

She gave me a look that made my satisfying moment go up in a puff of smoke. But I kept trying. I never stopped trying.

She asked us to call the police often. At this point in her disease, she was not capable of tracking down a number for the police station, and I questioned how capable she was of making a phone call to anyone. Months earlier, she could call her oldest sister or her friends. Now no longer able to get them on the line, she only spoke to people with my assistance. Tom and I did the best we could at convincing her that the police were working on getting the men out of her bed and out of her room forever. But when the police weren't getting the job done fast enough, she decided that it was time to contact the government.

"Tom, you know people. Why don't you write a letter to the housing authority?" she pleaded.

"What housing authority, Francesca?" he replied.

"Ask them if they can do something about these men. Get them out of the house. Really. You own this house, and they don't have the right to be here. You should tell someone."

"OK, I'll call them tomorrow."

But the very next day, we resumed the practice we did every night. Tom yelled at them to get out of the room, just as we did with the monsters in our children's bedrooms many years ago. It seemed to quiet the hallucinations long enough for her to actually get in the bed—but not long enough to sleep through the night comfortably. They always returned.

Bedtime became a ritual that started at four o'clock, when she began to sundown. She ate a big lunch and never liked a big dinner, so I typically gave her a plate of snack food. Olives, cheese, fruit, crackers, or tapas. At five o'clock, Tom would get her a tiny glass of red wine and a little bag of oyster crackers—the kind you get with soup at a restaurant. Mom's bugs were not only consuming her bedroom, they were consuming all her food as well, so I bought as many individually wrapped items as I could possibly find. In a normal environment, it's not the cheapest way to shop, but when you consider the amount of food she threw away because it was "full of bugs," it was considerably cheaper!

Mom and Tom watched TV while she sipped her small glass of wine and flossed her teeth. I took the opportunity to sit outside and write in my journal, read, or chat on the phone. If the Boston Red Sox were on, she would last until seven thirty, but she would tire of the news by seven o'clock and start wandering. She would get up and go plug in her electric blanket and then return to her chair for five or ten minutes. Then she'd get up again to go brush her teeth and return to her chair, then get up and go into the kitchen for a little walk. Each time she moved straight ahead. No turning, no pivoting, no changing directions—making the loop around the entire house into the kitchen and back through the living room to her bedroom that was just steps behind her designated chair in the living room. At that point, Tom would stick his head out the door.

"She's wandering."

"Ready for bed, Mom?" I asked.

"I think so," she replied.

I helped her change into her nightclothes; then I piled up her pillows. She had had the same pillows for at least thirty years, and they were as thin as a pillow could possibly get. I took her four pillows, folded them in half, and piled them high at the head of her bed just how she liked it.

"Yertle the Turtle," I said every night.

And every night, she giggled as if it were the first time she had heard it.

I pulled back the blankets so she could get into bed. She started on her hands and knees. Slowly she got herself onto the bed as I gently put my hand on her bottom to guide her. When she was good and ready, she began to crawl toward the middle of the bed as I counted...one, two, three, four, fi—and then she stopped.

"Come on, Mom. You can do eight."

Sometimes she stopped to flick away a bug; sometimes she stopped because she was getting too close to whomever was on the other side of the bed. If it was the latter, I went around and without saying a word, swiped my hands across the bed to signal it was OK to continue and then returned to the other side to start again.

"Five," she said.

"Six, seven," I continued.

"OK, one more big one—eight."

She completely let herself go, flopping onto her back and knocking down a pillow or two. I picked up her upper body and while holding her in place, piled the pillows back up and then placed her onto them.

"How's that?" I asked.

"That's good," she mumbled.

I walked across to the other side of the bed to unplug the electric blanket before I returned to the other side to turn on her nightlight. "Are you all set?" I asked.

"Yes."

"Are you too close to the edge of the bed?"

"No, if I have to use the bathroom, it's best if I have a front-row seat."

I stood by her for a minute or two, giving her time to process her thoughts in case she had a question about the following day's agenda. We did that every night for over a year. When she got up in the middle of the night, it was too difficult for her to get all the way back into bed on her own, so she extended her arms out, grabbed a corner, and pulled herself onto the bed on her belly, where she stayed until morning.

She typically woke around ten o'clock. The previous year, I let her make her own bed. I thought the activity was good for her, so I let her do the chore on days when the schedule was clear. What took me three minutes to do took her thirty with all the distractions along the way. Misplaced items became gifts from unknown friends. A used tissue taken from the box by her bed during the night transformed into an origami message by morning.

"Who would leave an origami message in your bed?" I asked.

"Oh, I don't know. Probably that man. I think he likes me," she said with a giggle.

"Hmmmm." I wondered why she didn't say that in anger.

She made her way to the kitchen and sat in her favorite spot. I gave her one piece of toast with an individual jar of jam or jelly like you get at a hotel and a little espresso spoon to spread it. I served her coffee in a china teacup with a tiny pitcher of cream on the side. I used antique salts as tiny glass bowls to put her pills in, one before food and another after she ate. While she munched on her toast, I added another plate with something sweet—a slice of coffee cake or a mini éclair. Not only was it fancy and dainty, it was easier for her to handle. Anything big or bulky would result in a spill, which embarrassed her.

Where I mastered the art of kindness at bedtime and breakfast, I completely failed at showering. The bars we'd installed in her shower months earlier were no longer sufficient; now she needed bars on one side and a person holding her up on the other. Mom was a consummate cleaner, constantly decluttering and organizing. Like my grandmother, I preferred gardening to cleaning any day. But Mom saw no sense in gardening when there were plenty of grocery stores about. Besides, it was dirty! Cleaning was what she liked to do—even while on her way to the shower. I showered her three times a week—and I dreaded it each and every time.

For me, the procedure entailed getting her completely undressed while running the water until it was just the right temperature so it wouldn't need to be adjusted once she was under the stream. One of the symptoms of LBD that Mom had was extreme sensitivity to fluctuations in temperatures, so we couldn't risk the water warming or cooling once she got under it.

"OK, Mom, let's get in," I said every time, as if it were the first.

For her, the procedure was taking her time. She took one step closer to the shower.

"Come on, Mom. The water is just how you like it."

She took another two steps and then stopped to clean out a drawer.

"Ready, Mom?"

She took another step and then stopped again to inventory her box of toiletries, making sure she had everything she needed.

"Come *on*, Mom!"

She took one more look at herself in the mirror.

"Finally!"

She was in.

Before every shower, Mom took ten minutes to take five steps.

When she was done showering, I was eager to get her out and dry her off, thinking about the countless other things I had to do. "You ready to get out?"

"No wait; I want to drip off a little."

I would stand and watch her drip for three minutes before insisting she'd dripped enough so I could help her out of the shower. I handed her the deodorant, and she applied it herself, while I applied lotion to her back, arms, and legs, and then dressed her. My patience waned with each shower, like a phase of the moon. I reassured myself it only took about forty-five minutes from start to finish, so I told myself to bite my tongue, take a deep breath, and carry on—until the day came when she began having toileting issues, and I needed her to get in the shower unscheduled and fast.

"OK, Mom, let's get in," I insisted.

She took one step closer to the shower.

"Come on, Mom; the water is just how you like it."

She stopped to clean out a drawer.

"You've got to get in that shower, Mom. You have poop everywhere!"

She stopped again to inventory her box of toiletries, making sure she had everything she needed.

"Come *on*, Mom. Please get in the shower! We can do that later."

I was trying not to offend her, but I couldn't stand it another minute. I ran out of the bathroom to breathe in clean air.

She stopped to look in the mirror.

"Mom, get in the shower—now!" I said when I returned to the bathroom.

"Peggy, it's no different than someone smoking a cigarette."

Now she's going to give me a lesson on what smells worse? Now, as she's standing in the middle of the bathroom, soiled, water running, patience waning? I lost it.

"Mom, get in the friggin' shower!" I screamed.

She did.

After that particular shower, I felt extreme remorse. Did I think for one minute she wouldn't have cleaned herself up if she could have? Did I think for one minute she wouldn't have showered herself if she could have? I was just sorry it had to get to that point before I figured it out. But figure it out I did, and I hired someone to shower her the very next day. Debbie came on Monday, Wednesday, and Saturday mornings to shower and dress my mother. I could hear them on the baby monitor while up in my room. Debbie the shower angel took my most dreaded task and turned it into a party! They had a grand time with clothes, makeup, hair curlers, coffee, pastries, and conversations about old times, fashion, and men. They got along so well, I hired Debbie to spend more time with her.

Elder Services provided Mom with a companion who came and sat with her for three hours a week. Natalie came on Wednesdays from three in the afternoon and stayed until six at night. I took that time to see my therapist three times a month and ran errands on the fourth. Once Debbie entered our lives, I had her stay after the Wednesday shower until Natalie the companion relieved her at three. That gave me one whole day a week to do what I needed to do, and sometimes I was even able to grab an early dinner with Tom.

Every so often, my mother would tell me that we shouldn't have Debbie come to shower her. Not because she didn't like her company, but because she didn't want to accept the fact that she needed help, especially to anyone beyond the doors that permitted her to deceive herself. In her mind, if she acknowledged she needed help, she acknowledged not being able to live alone. And that meant no more winters in Florida. I fashioned a number of creative lies to bring in outside help without bruising her ego and breaking her spirit. In this case, I told her Debbie needed the money. When she told me she didn't need my friend's daughter to come and sit with her on the rare occasion Tom and I went out at night, I told her she needed community service for her college application. Honesty always hurt her deeply and usually ended in a battle that neither of us won.

Mom could go days being able to dress herself correctly, although it took hours; then one day, she would come out of her room with her shirt on upside down, not understanding why it didn't fit properly. One day she would be able to put her sneakers on to go for a walk (although it took an hour), and other days I would find her sneakers off to the side of her chair with the shoelaces completely pulled out of the shoes. She couldn't figure out how to turn the stove on but could hold a conversation with you about world politics and family issues. She couldn't make a phone call, but she could tell you who was scheduled to pitch the Red Sox game, the names and ages of everyone important to her, and current events that interested her.

The constant struggle to get through the day with her was taking a toll on me, not only as a daughter losing bits of her mother, but as a caregiver losing bits of herself. I received a grant from a local dementia support institution—a $500 gift certificate for in-home caregiving—which gave me three and a half nights out with Tom, but who's counting! We used one of those nights to attend a fundraising gala at Tom's place of employment, where we were chatting with his colleague and his wife.

"We should have dinner together. Tom and I will have you to our house since it's difficult for me to get out," I decided.

"Great idea," Tom agreed.

"Not this coming Saturday—but the next," I said.

"OK! It's a date," they said.

"I'll make homemade raviolis," I said.

"We'll bring some Vietnamese spring rolls," they replied.

"Perfect!"

~

Sitting on the deck in my bathing suit two Saturdays later, after a swim in our pool, I heard a knock on the door.

"Hello," Tom said with surprise.

I heard chatter in the background. *Surely he'll send them away,* I thought.

"Peggy," he yelled. "Guess who's here?"

"Oh my God, Tom, who?" I gasped as he walked out onto the deck with our invited guests.

155

Anyone who has been to my house for dinner will tell you I'm a fanatic. I use real dishes, never plastic. I use real linen, real silverware, and real glassware, even with children—and even if there are eighty guests coming. I am completely organized, with appetizers, wine, sparkling water, dinner warming, dessert cooling, clean house, candles lit, and music on low. I am dressed and ready to greet my guests at least thirty minutes before they are expected to arrive, just in case they are early, so they won't feel any discomfort. And yet on this day when my invited guests came through the door, I was sitting on the deck in total disarray, with an untidy house, no food, wine, water, linens, glasses, silver, appetizers, makeup, or clothes! Totally and completely mortified, I screamed and ran past them as quickly as I could in hopes that they didn't see me—which of course they did. They looked at me dazed and confused, as if they'd just stepped into a scene from *The Twilight Zone.*

"What is going on with you?" I said to myself as I stood in my bedroom, trying to find my mind.

"I don't even remember inviting them!"

"How did this happen?" The one-way conversation continued.

"Get it together, Peggy."

"What the hell is wrong with you? Why can't you remember?"

As I stood there trying to put the pieces together, I quickly realized my private therapy session would have to wait. I needed to focus on the issue at hand—the guests downstairs who were hungry and utterly confused!

"They'll understand," I told myself. "Get dressed and get it together."

While Tom and our guests munched on the delicious homemade spring rolls they brought, I pulled together a dinner from the freezer. Somehow we managed to have a wonderful time and would laugh the blunder away. At the end of the day, I realized I should no longer plan my life too far in advance and made a conscious decision to stop entertaining guests in my home—at least for the time being.

THIRTEEN

You never know what can happen.

—Francesca Jean

With the physical work of preparing meals, dressing her, numerous loads of daily laundry to wash away the bugs and cat pee, taking her on daily walks or weekly appointments, and the emotional toll of figuring out what she was trying to say, along with my own breaking heart, I was constantly tired. But a huge contributor to my fatigue did not come from actively running around—it was emotional. I was so tired that I often tuned out what was going on around me in order to preserve my sanity. One afternoon, a few of us were gathered around watching television. My mother was in her chair, I was on the couch, and my three grandsons on the floor were multitasking between Legos and cartoons. A silly TV advertisement came on that struck me funny, causing me to giggle. Before I knew it, I had lost control, and I continued to giggle until tears streamed down my face. My grandchildren looked up from their creations, stared at me for a minute, and then burst into laughter. I laughed at them laughing at me, who laughed at me laughing at them. Like an impromptu jam session with each of us singing a song of unscripted emotions, the volume rose to a new level. Mom sat quietly in her chair until she could no longer resist joining the group.

"Cock-a-doodle-doo!" she said in a long, loud, singsong, quite-pleased-with-herself voice.

The absurdity of the scene fueled the laughter as it continued to fill the room. Mom thought we were "cuckoo," but Lewy couldn't find the right word.

Mom was exhausted as well. After the hospital and rehab visit late in the summer of 2013, my mother was never fully able to resume her life as she knew it. She had trouble keeping track of time, days, and appointments. She could no longer make sense of her calendar book, so Tom made a weekly schedule template with a section for her and a section for me. I made copies, and every Sunday I posted a new one on the refrigerator. My section had appointments with my therapist, things to do for her (pedicures, hair appointments, and family commitments), while hers were filled with visiting medical people, Debbie the shower angel, and random lunch dates with family or friends. With the exception of my appointments with my therapist, all the appointments were for Mom, although in point of fact they were all for me. Her appointments were my appointments too; she was no longer able to attend these meetings on her own. But seeing her name on the schedule gave her a distorted sense of independence and productivity, so she looked at it twenty times a day, and we discussed each entry ten times a day.

She also had trouble with the toilet—both physically and mentally. Some days she didn't need any help at all; other days she simply couldn't figure out what to do.

"I can't find the pipe that comes out of the top of the toilet," she said.

"What pipe?" I asked.

"You know, the mechanism."

"OK, come with me. We'll figure it out together."

She followed me into the bathroom, where I gave her step-by-step instructions.

"First you stand in front of the toilet with your back facing it. Then you take your pants down, all the way down. Then you sit," I instructed.

"But what about the mechanism?" she asked again.

"Don't worry about that yet. That's last," I answered.

"Oh, OK."

"Then you pee. Then you wipe. Then you get up and pull your pants up," I continued.

"Oh, OK," she said.

"Now you flush," I said.

"Oh, good."

"Here, back here is the mechanism that you use to flush. Just push it down."

"Oh, so that's how you do it?"

"Yep, it's easy."

Days later, she would ask about the mechanism again and need another lesson.

Every time she went to sit, she always swung to her left, missing half the seat and peeing on the floor—then blaming it on the cat or insisting the toilet leaked! Every aide, therapist, companion, nurse, and loved one worked with her to get her to sit straight because they were sure she would miss the chair and fall on the floor, but she never once sat straight and never fell on the floor. At the request of Debbie the shower angel, we bought her an elevated toilet seat with handles. The seat didn't do much to prevent the mess on the floor because she still swung to the left when she sat (we went through a lot of paper towels), but it was safer and that was comforting for everyone.

The disease was winning over Mom's ability to fight it. I did what I could do to keep her as healthy as possible and keep clear of two big threats—the UTI and constipation. I was careful with meal choices and vigilant with her daily prune treat. I warmed prune juice, added two cranberry pills and melted them, and then added two large prunes and crushed them up with a fork. Then I poured the thick mixture into a clear glass mug and topped it with a dollop of whipped cream. Most of the time, she would drink it; other times, she didn't, proclaiming she would "save it for later." But by the time "later" came around, it was "full of bugs," so she dumped it down the sink. Most of the time she would eat the pizza without cheese; other times she would eat the pizza with cheese. I walked an uncomfortable line of steering her in the right direction while giving her some space to make her own decisions, even if they were unhealthy ones. And I spent endless hours wishing she would just trust that everything I did was paramount to her well-being.

I also found ways for her to be helpful around the house, at least in her eyes. While she could no longer help with household chores, she had a dry mop in her bedroom that she took out a couple of times a day for a few minutes at a time to clean up. I also gave her the job of mating the socks when I was doing laundry. She was able to match up a couple each load, and that was enough for her to feel useful.

"Good job," I said as I took a pile of unmatched socks away.

I didn't fully realize how long she had gone without doing any house-work of her own until my friend Lizzy and I took a quick trip to the Florida condo in October 2013 to check things out. We literally spent four days cleaning that little tiny place from the minute we woke up until eleven o'clock at night. The only time we took to ourselves was one late af-ternoon lunch at a restaurant for two hours and one excursion to the community pool for two hours. Every other minute we spent cleaning or sleeping. Mom must have gone years without cleaning. I wondered why I didn't notice while I spent time there. I thought back to the previous year when I'd bought her a new vacuum cleaner because she couldn't handle her bigger, heavier machine. I remembered her bringing it out on occasion and leaving it in the middle of the room and then moving on to another task. As I assumed the job of vacuuming, I thought she just got distracted, but now I wonder if it was her intention all along. She only had so much energy to dole out during the day, so she became quite skilled at delegating without asking.

～

As fall turned to winter and the New England weather took on a cold, dark, and dreary look, my mother began to get more and more anxious and unsure. She had a difficult time portraying what she wanted to say—what was a dream, and what was real.

"How's Nancy?" she asked about her friend out of the blue.

"Why?" I asked.

"She was involved in some sort of car accident."

"How do you know that?" I was puzzled. She had very little access to the outside world without my knowing.

"I had a dream."

"Oh, it was just a dream?"

"Well, I don't know. Is she OK?"

"Mom, I don't know what you're trying to say."

"Well I'm not sure either, so let's just leave it at that."

She began to address me in conversation while looking in the opposite direction at one of her hallucinations, or maybe she wasn't even talking to me at all. I was never really sure. She also became obstinate about not following my instructions for keeping her healthy. The more she needed me, the more she fought me, especially around other people. She readily took my arm when we walked anywhere outside the home, but as soon as someone she knew came into view, she batted my arm away in an instant. Her denial made me sad, her hiding of the disease infuriated me, her determination to fight made me proud, and her tenacity exhausted me.

Then came the holidays. Thanksgiving was a happy holiday. I moved two tables together and set them for fourteen people, complete with china, crystal, linen, place cards, candles, and flowers. The table made a glorious statement. It took up the whole kitchen, and Mom was very happy to spend hours at the table eating and chatting while surrounded by her family and friends. But she still hated Christmas and refused to leave the house. That meant me staying home with her while sending Tom off to the traditional oysters-and-champagne brunch at our friend's home. I spent the day feeling sorry for myself.

"Look at those kids over there," she said as she pointed to a strand of green garland with Christmas lights.

"Yeah," I said, completely uninterested.

"They shouldn't be putting the lights in their mouths."

"No, they shouldn't."

After Christmas, things calmed down, and we settled into a reclusive routine of quiet days, fending off talk of Florida, and preparing Tom for his six-week voyage on the sea. My mother's behavior was a little more bizarre than normal, but I made excuses for her under the gloomy circumstances. To cheer us both up, I took her out to a lunch I arranged with a few friends I worked with for many years. It was a special restaurant where you dined for hours, and it was one of her favorite places. When lunch was over, we all walked out together. My friends stood with her in the lobby while I went to get the car to pick her up at the door.

"I'm not going," she insisted when I got out of the car to get her.

"What do you mean, Mom?" I asked.

"I'm not going back there."

"We're going home."

"*No!* I'm not going."

I gently tried to reason with her while the others watched, but she wasn't having any of it. I began to get frustrated and embarrassed. "Please get in the car, Mom."

"No!"

"Mom, we're going straight home."

"I'm not going."

"Get in the *car!*" I said as I physically walked her to the front seat.

"I'm so sorry, Peggy," said my friend Sheila.

I glanced over to my friends with tears in my eyes.

I hated this! *This is not the relationship I want to have with my mother,* I thought. I could see each one of my friends reading my mind as if the words escaped into a thought bubble.

The new year came and brought with it snow, ice, and freezing cold, making it impossible to take my mother out for even a few hours a week. Tom left mid-January, and her bizarre behavior increased, but again I thought it was due to the change in our household and the fact that she always felt safer with a man in the house. She was confused, wandered a lot, and had conversations with her hallucinations. She played peek-a-boo with the little hallucinations hiding under the table, complained about the cat and birds, and screamed at the men in her bed.

And about a week after Tom's departure, all hell broke loose.

She had been complaining about being constipated for days—and during those days, I did everything in my power to help the situation. She refused the powder laxative (the container had bugs in it). I made her mixtures of prune juice with chunks of prunes, but she wouldn't drink any of them because she thought I added the powdered laxative with the bugs in it. Three days went by with our entire focus of discussion and attention on how to get her to poop. One morning, I went into her bathroom to see her eating a laxative in the form of a chocolate bar. Knowing how drug sensitive she was and not knowing how much she ate, I grabbed it from her before she could put any more in her system. I threw it away, and we waited. Sure enough, by that afternoon, she could not control her diarrhea, nor could I! For two days, I cleaned up after her and chased her around the house, trying to change her clothes and shower her while I waited for a call back from her doctor. When it was all said and done, I filled five large trash bags with clothes, towels, facecloths, and bathmats. Once again, the doctor didn't have anything available right away. On morning four of "D" week, I showered her, showered myself, and took her to the ER.

"She has Lewy body disease," I said to the triage nurse.

"She has what?" she replied.

"She has Lewy body disease," I said to the nurse in the ER.

"Lewy who?" she replied.

"She has Lewy body disease," I said to the doctor.

He nodded blankly.

"She has Lewy body disease," I said to the nurse who relieved the previous nurse.

"What? How do you spell that?" he replied.

"She's pill sensitive. You can't give LBD patients the same drugs you give others," I told anyone who would listen.

She was diagnosed with colitis and a UTI and was admitted. I thought after the last visit, they would have LEWY BODY in big letters on her chart and that everyone who treated her would know all about her disease and act accordingly. I was sure everyone who cared for her would treat her appropriately. It was only six months after the last visit, so I was sure they would give her proper care. I was very sure. But just to be *really* sure, before I left the hospital at the end of the day, I hunted down the head hospitalist and the ER cardiologist to inform them as reinforcement. Just to be sure.

The next morning, I went in to see her, and she looked good. Treatment was simple—a stool softener for the blockage and antibiotics for the UTI. I ran into her case manager in the corridor, and she gave me a choice. Would I prefer she go to rehab after her stay, or would I like to take her home and have visiting medical professionals come for about an hour or two each day? With no help at home and no desire to deal with her while she had a UTI, I opted for rehab. I left her caseworker and went to the café to get her something to eat. I brought coffee and a muffin back to her room, and we ate breakfast together. She was madder than a wet hen—but only at me. When someone came in to visit her, she turned on the charm and was sweet as pie. But as soon as they left, she resumed being nasty to her caregiver, her daughter, who was "betraying her by making her stay in the hospital."

"This disease is a farce!" she hissed.

"I'm sorry, Mom, but you don't help matters."

"Why are you leaving me here?"

"Because you need to be treated."

"You wouldn't believe the things that go on in this hospital—you wouldn't!"

"You make this so hard."

"Don't leave me here."

I tried to comfort her, reason with her, and sympathize with her, but she wouldn't listen. My head kept telling me it was her UTI and the hallucinations and to be patient with her, but my heart was growing heavy. Having had all this caregiving daughter could take of her attitude toward me, I left her at three o'clock that afternoon. I made a stop at the nurses' station on my way out.

"She has Lewy body disease," I said to the person standing there.

"She has what?" she answered back.

"Lewy body disease. It means she can't take certain drugs."

"OK."

I walked down the corridor, went down the elevator, and out the door.

Taking advantage of my newfound freedom, I called my friend Diane and met her for a late lunch/early dinner. Shortly after sitting down with my date, I received a call from the hospital.

"Hi. I'm calling to tell you that your mother is out of control. She wants to go home. She's really strong—"

All 115 pounds of her, I thought.

"And is hurting people, so we gave her Haldol to calm her down, but we thought if she could just talk with you, maybe it would help."

"You gave her *what*?" I asked as I made my way out of the dining room and into the lobby.

"We gave her Haldol. She had a 'no Ativan' on her chart."

"She should have a 'no Haldol' on there too!"

"We gave it to her about an hour ago. She's fine."

"You're not supposed to give Lewy body patients Haldol. I told the woman at the nurses' station before I left. I told *everyone* I saw. How did you not get that message?"

"Will you talk with her?" she asked in an attempt to get rid of me and my rant.

"Yes, please," I answered trying to calm down as she transferred my call.

"Seventh floor, may I help you?"

"Someone is trying to transfer me to my mother," I answered.

"Hold on; I'll transfer you."

I did my best to remain calm.

"Hello?" a voice said.

"Someone is trying to transfer me to my mother."

"Oh, yes." The entire seventh floor was privy to what was going on in Mom's room.

Breathe and stay calm, I told myself.

"Hello. I'm here with your mother. I will hand the phone to her."

The nurse handed the phone to my mother, and she threw it right back at her. She refused to talk to me.

I cut my dinner date short and returned home early enough to make a phone call to my mother's case manager before she left for the day. I took the opportunity to educate her on LBD and drug intake. I told her I warned many, many people, on many, many occasions—and the information continued to fall on deaf ears.

"I think I'm going to file a report," she said.

"That's good; hopefully that will help," I replied, completely misunderstanding what that meant.

"I'm going to send out a mass e-mail as well, and I'll bring it up at the morning meeting."

"Oh, that's wonderful. Thank you."

"Would you like me to transfer you to your mother's room?"

"Yes, that would be great, and thank you for all your help."

"You're welcome."

She then transferred me to the nurses' station, where again I took the opportunity to explain to the person who answered about LBD and drug intake. She told me she would have the doctor call me back—but that never happened. I was, however, able to speak with my mother, and she did sound coherent, which made me feel better and thankfully halted an unwanted trip to the hospital that night. Being alone, I had plenty of time to spend that evening thinking about the conversation with Mom's case manager.

"This is a good thing," I said to myself.

Finally, someone would actually *listen* to what I had to say. *They would be so impressed with my knowledge*, I thought, *and so excited to learn about this disease.*

～

The next morning, I got up really early and printed off some information from the lbd.org website. I sat at the kitchen table sipping my coffee as I practiced my imaginary question-and-answer session and polishing up my speech. I was quite pleased with myself. After showering, I dug out my best serious-but-casual clothes, put my hair in curlers, and put on some makeup. I was sure they would praise me for the sundowning bag that I filled with distractions of little bags of crackers, lottery scratch tickets, a toothbrush, and candy. I just knew they were going to ask me to speak at all the workshops that they would be hosting. The head nurse will call staff members of all varieties to tell them I've arrived so they can have the opportunity to come and talk with me directly. Oh, how they would love hearing my stories and listening to my knowledge of this Lewy body disease that so many people knew nothing about. As I walked out the door, I was prepared for an incredibly satisfying day, and for the first time in months, I actually looked presentable!

But to my complete surprise, that wasn't what happened at all. In fact, just the opposite occurred. No one would speak to me—hell, no one would even look at me!

"Did you hear?" one nurse said to the other until we locked eyes.

I turned away and walked closer to Mom's room.

"Her daughter called the caseworker—you know, 704 with Lewy body disease," I heard a nurse say on her cell phone as she wheeled her cart down the corridor. People literally turned and walked the other way when they realized who I was. People who I interacted with previously, now just stared at me when I said "Good morning." I realized my good intentions weren't so good afterall.

I stood there flabbergasted, my mouth open. It brought back a memory of the time John and Daniel got up early one morning and decided it would be fun to empty cereal boxes onto the floor and then slide through piles of Cheerios and Raisin Bran in their footed pajamas. These one- and two-year-old boys were having a grand time, until I came into the kitchen and yelled.

"Whoa, whoa, whoa! What is going on here? No! We don't do that with food!"

They looked at me with that same confused expression. Clearly, I was as mistaken as the boys were about how things were done.

I snapped out of my euphoria, looked around, and walked in the room to see my mother sitting in a chair, fully dressed. The nurse tending to her told me that the doctor wanted to discharge her that day and have me give her antibiotics by mouth.

"She went all night without antibiotics because she ripped out her IV and refused another," she said.

No johnny? All night without antibiotics? I thought to myself.

"I'm not staying here," Mom chimed in.

I was stunned. My head had so many thoughts spinning around that I developed a headache. I couldn't complete one thought before being hit with another. I was overloaded. Mom hadn't been there long enough for insurance to pay for rehab. She was nasty and uncooperative. What was I going to do? The hospital walls appeared to be growing in size around me, or maybe I was shrinking.

"Peggy, get me out of here," she begged.

I couldn't respond. I couldn't breathe.

"I'm *not* staying here!" she yelled.

I walked out of the room and down to the end of the now-massive hallway to a spot where I could still see Mom sitting in her chair, but was sure she couldn't identify me. I felt very small and insignificant. I held on to the railing that lined the wall, steadied myself, and started to sob when the elevator door opened in front of me.

"Hello, Peggy." It was Mom's caseworker.

"Hi," I said through my tears.

"What's going on? Are you OK?"

"They want to discharge my mother."

"They can't. She needs to stay three days, or she can't go to rehab."

"Is it because I called you?" She paused for a moment but didn't acknowledge my question.

"I'll get physical therapy to do an evaluation on her. The doctors always listen to what they recommend."

I walked a little closer to Mom's room when I heard the nurse call PT over the loudspeaker.

"Where do you live?" asked the physical therapist as he squatted down to meet Mom in the chair.

"I don't!" she replied.

I interpreted that response as a dig to me because I wouldn't take her home.

"Can you stand up?" the therapist asked.

She didn't respond, so he helped her stand, and the two of them went for a walk down the corridor in the opposite direction and back to her room while I retreated back to my spot at the other end.

He helped Mom back into her chair; then he walked across the hall to the nurses' station and spoke to the person behind the desk loudly enough for me to hear. "She most definitely needs therapy. I recommend you keep her overnight."

I closed my eyes and said a quiet prayer of thanks.

Still standing in the hallway, I called an acquaintance whom I met at a support group. She managed to calm me down a bit, and we set up an appointment to meet for lunch the following day. I also reached out to my "sister" the nurse, who told me she believed it would be best to remove myself from the situation and go home, especially if I wasn't getting a warm and fuzzy feeling from the people caring for Mom. I went to the nurses' station, handed the papers I printed off with the LBD information to the person standing there, and told them I was leaving—and would not be back.

"I will meet up with my mother tomorrow—at the nursing home," I whispered.

I walked into the nursing home the following morning and had a completely different greeting. The nurse on duty noticed that my mother was more agitated than usual, so she reviewed her chart and saw the notes from her neurologist.

"Peggy, I saw that the neurologist ordered Seroquel for your mom," said Nora.

"Seroquel?" I inquired.

"Yes, it's the brand name for Quetiapine."

"Oh, he did? I did some research, but I'm afraid about monitoring proper doses."

"We can do that for you. She's having a hard time, and I think it may help her."

"That would be so great. Let me think about it, and I'll let you know in the morning."

As I gave it some thought, I recalled the words my cousin Farah told me months earlier: "Do your research, empower yourself, and when you have to make a tough decision again, make it your own."

It was the perfect opportunity for her to have the drug administered properly and at the same time have someone observe her twenty-four hours a day. The next day I visited with my mother for a few hours and saw that she was struggling, so before I left, I stopped at the nurses' station and gave them the green light. A small dose of Seroquel proved to be helpful in calming my mom's fears without any side effects at all. Although the treatment was not successful in totally eliminating her hallucinations, she seemed more at peace.

Before Mom was to be discharged, I had a meeting with the heads of staff in the conference room at the nursing home, where the big question crept out onto the table.

"Do you want to bring her home, or do you want her to stay long term?" Nora asked.

"I'm not ready for long-term care, and God knows *she* wants to come home with me," I replied.

I had been thinking about it for months. That question that my children asked me about constantly. That question Tom and I had discussed at great length, and more significantly, just a few days earlier. While it would make our lives a whole lot easier, when push came to shove, neither Tom nor I were ready for her to go into long-term nursing care. She didn't want it, and we just couldn't bring ourselves to do it, even if it meant putting our own lives on hold for a while longer. We hoped that the Seroquel would continue to diminish her hallucinations, and we discussed ways to bring in more resources and give us some precious alone time.

With my mother safe in the same nursing home she had been to before, with people who loved her and took great care of her, it was time for me to find some respite. Tom was going to be in port in Florida and persuaded me to take a trip down to visit him. Multiple factors had to fall into place in order for me to venture off to see him. I had no intentions of chasing a ship around all alone, so I prayed for guidance. Once again, my prayers were answered, as my cousin Bella would be close by with her husband, JP, to help. I booked a trip, stayed with them for a few days, and stayed with Tom a few more. Grateful for the opportunity to get away and clear my head, I headed back to New England.

A week later Tom, Mom, and I were all home and left to figure out how to live with our new normal.

FOURTEEN

Every woman should have four husbands: one to earn the money; one who is good with the kids; one who is handy around the house; and one for sex.

—FRANCESCA JEAN

MOM LIVED WITH Tom and me for thirty years, and it was truly our wish to have her living with us until the day she died, but that wish was getting more difficult to fulfill with each passing month. Her denial of having the disease and declaring in countless ways that there was no reason for her (or anyone else, for that matter) to adapt to the situation was challenging. Everyone involved has to make adjustments when dealing with an illness, but it becomes tremendously burdensome when the patient refuses to cooperate.

Is she just being stubborn, or is the disease guiding her delusion? I wondered. *Would an earlier diagnosis have made a difference with her approach to dealing with the situation?*

I did know her well enough to realize that asking for help meant acknowledging her disease, and that was something she couldn't face head-on. Her needs were well taken care of, but her wants necessitated communication and asking for help. If I gave a small bag of oyster crackers to my three-year-old grandchild, she would spend a minute or two trying to open it. Once she inevitably realized that she needed help, she would hand it back to me to open it for her. If I gave my mother an unopened bag of oyster crackers, she would shake it, take two corners and move them back and forth in opposite directions, shake it again, and ultimately abandon it on her table. She wouldn't ask for help, she didn't want medication, and she certainly didn't think she needed to see a neurologist!

How many times throughout my life did I hear, "Don't tell me if there's something wrong with me, Peggy. I don't want to know." What an awful burden to put on a child—even if that child is an adult. She would help me in every aspect of my life, with anything I needed as a child, with my marriage, raising children, dealing with friendships, chores, and advice, but she wouldn't help me help her.

The second and final visit with her neurologist was in early March 2014. Once again, she refused to go, saying that there was nothing wrong with her and that he was a quack. At this point in our journey, I really didn't think a neurologist could help. I wasn't sure if there was anything anyone could do to help her. It was like we were whitewater rafting, halfway down the river, and we just had to make it to the other end. Somehow I managed to get her into the car that afternoon, but she was not pleased. She refused to get out of the car when we arrived at the office. The medical facility was fairly new and quite impressive. It was a long two-story building that had doctors' offices, a walk-in clinic, a rehabilitation component, and a hospice unit.

"Why do I have to live here?" she asked.

"No, Mom, you're not going to live here; we're just here for a doctor's appointment," I replied.

"How could you do this to me?"

"It's just a doctor's appointment."

"I don't want to stay here."

"You're not staying here."

"I'll find someone else who will take me in."

"*Mom*, I'm not leaving you here. It's just a doctor's appointment."

It didn't matter how many times or in how many ways I told her it was simply a doctor's visit; she couldn't hear it. I stood firm and used my best authoritative voice to get her out of the car. Getting from the car to the building was much easier, as it was simply too cold to stop and argue, especially for someone with Lewy body disease who refused to wear proper winter apparel. She looked adorable, though!

Within minutes, we were sitting in the doctor's exam room. He came in with a smile. "How are you doing?" he asked.

"She's throwing me out!" she said as she pointed to me with her thumb, like she was trying to hitch a ride from a stranger.

"She thinks we're checking her into long-term care," I said.

"Oh no," he said with a calming voice. "This is just a visit."

She sat there with her arms crossed and a mean scowl on her face.

"Can I help you take your jacket off?" he asked.

"No," she said.

"I'd like to listen to your heart."

"No!" she repeated.

He asked her a few more questions, but she refused to even look at him, let alone answer him. And that was about the gist of it.

"Call me if you need anything," he said as we left the exam room.

Well, that went just as I expected.

What I didn't expect was for her to give me a hard time about returning home. She stood in the lobby refusing to leave the building and refusing to leave with me. I eventually got her into the car, but she was tremendously upset and lost control of her reasoning skills. She was confused and convinced I was dropping her off at some facility for good. She couldn't even see the familiar surroundings leading her home to the place where she desperately wanted to stay. She was like a scared little kitten, and as we drove home, my heart grew heavy with sadness.

How could I ever bring myself to take her to long-term care outside my home? All I wanted to do was get her into her familiar surroundings, light a fire in the fireplace, get her in comfortable clothes, and put her in her chair in front of the TV, with some food and a cup of hot chocolate. But doing so took hours because even her familiar surroundings were not familiar that afternoon, and she fought me every step of the way.

How could I have done something so cruel to her? I asked myself over and over.

She sat in her chair with her body twisted off to the side and didn't say a word for hours. I tried to talk with her and clarify the events of the afternoon, but it was clear she didn't want anything to do with me or my explanation. In her mind, I had betrayed her. Later on, when Tom came home from work, I told him what happened, and he agreed to talk with her.

"How's it going, Francesca?" he asked as he knelt down to be at her level.

"Why can't I go to Florida?" she asked.

"Well, you can't go because you have a disease and you can't take care of yourself."

"What? The same disease that my sister has?"

"Yes, we think so."

She took a long pensive pause. "I'm disgusted with myself," she said. "This is exactly what I didn't want to happen," she added.

"What didn't you want to happen?" he asked quietly.

"I didn't want to be like a two-year-old!"

With heavy hearts, we left her alone with her thoughts for a few minutes before resuming our nighttime ritual.

～

A week later, she sat in that same chair with the same twisted body off to the side when Tom came home from work.

"She's not speaking to me again. Will you try talking to her?" I asked

"How are you doing today, Francesca?" Tom asked.

"I want to go home," she said.

"You are home."

The two of them settled into their evening ritual of watching TV while she munched on her dinner and sipped her water. An hour later, she spoke again. "Would you please take me home now?" she said.

"Francesca, you *are* home!" he replied.

"No! No!" she said loudly.

"Look, this is your chair. This is your TV. This is your home."

"I want to go home!"

Now sitting at attention and turning the volume down on the television, Tom tried to engage her in conversation, but she was too upset. I came into the room and stood in the background to see if he could talk her down without my intervening, but she didn't come around.

"Please, I want to go home."

He knelt down beside her.

"Pine Street. I want to go to Pine Street," she said.

"You are on Pine Street. You're home."

"Please! Please?" she begged. "If you do this, I will never ask you for anything else ever again. I just want you to take me home. *Please!* Please take me home."

"OK, let's go. I'll take you home," Tom replied.

He slowly got her in the car and took her for a ride. They rode around for about ten minutes before he brought her back.

"Thank you!" she said.

She sat down in the same chair she was in ten minutes earlier, but this time she was home.

Mom began having even greater difficulties with time and appointments. She had her own calendar book in her room, which she repeatedly brought out to the kitchen to cross-check with her weekly scheduled appointments on the refrigerator, but very often, her appointment book was opened on the wrong month. She looked for verbal confirmation constantly.

"What time is my appointment?" she asked.

"Noon," I answered, but the information wasn't helpful.

"So how long do I have before we go?"

"One hour."

"OK." That was the information she was looking for.

I scheduled appointments after noon so she would have time to get ready, but not too long after noon because she would grow more anxious as the day progressed. And I definitely wanted to have her home and in bedtime clothes by five o'clock—preferably four o'clock to be ready for sundowning. Weekly scheduling soon became too overwhelming for her to process, so we stopped using that format and changed to a daily plan. One piece of paper on the refrigerator with the plan of the day was all she could process. Gone were all the photos, magnets, drawings by my grandchildren, and anything else that would distract her from her intended attempt to simply see what was on the schedule for that day.

On April 15, 2014, my father came back into our lives. He had been diagnosed with cancer nine months earlier while living with my brother Tim in a nearby state. Shortly after Christmas, Tim, another sailor, left for the other side of the world, leaving my father at his home to fend for himself with outside help. My father was quite capable of taking care of himself physically, but as it turned out, not so much emotionally. One of his friends told me he would go long periods of time without grooming himself and often didn't get out of bed until after noon, which was unusual because it didn't matter at what time or in what condition my father went to bed, he was always up and about before 7:00 a.m.

Shortly after Tim left, the phone calls started coming my way, along with a nasty e-mail *telling* me to step up to the plate by a distant family member.

Why is everything my responsibility by default? What if I had never been born? Would my parents' care be someone else's responsibility? Figure it out over there. I'm busy here, I thought.

After fuming for a few hours, I realized that there was no room in my world for any repulsive behavior. Therapy taught me to release all those negative feelings, so that's what I did; I deleted it and dismissed it. I sympathized with the people who were caring for him, but I couldn't take on the role as his caregiver, as my hands were busy with my mother.

My father eventually ended up in the hospital with failure to thrive. From there, he went into a rehabilitation facility, and he began to call me daily. Each time he called, I told him I could not have him come live with me but would do whatever I could to make arrangements for him to live closer to me; that way, I could help with his care without taking on the entire task. But that wasn't good enough for my father, so he had his friend Frederick check him out of the nursing home and into Fred's home. And, of course, that didn't last long. My father, who thought he was the nicest guy in the world, honestly couldn't figure out why after a few short weeks, no one wanted him as a houseguest. So after said few short weeks, he started calling me—every day. And when he didn't call, Frederick did! I reiterated my offer to relocate him to my area—but not to my home.

"I mean it, Dad. I can't have you living here," I insisted.

"I know," he replied.

"I've told you a hundred times because I mean it. You can't live here."

"I got it."

"All right then. I'll get working on relocating you to a nursing home really close to me."

"OK, baby. Thanks."

I spoke with his hospice caseworker, who told me his diagnosis was grim and that he had about one month to live. Together we transferred him over to a local hospice agency while I worked on getting him state-funded Medicaid. I also worked with the nursing home admissions to get him out of Fred's home and nearer to me as quickly as possible, but I knew full well it could take six weeks or more. My father's daily calls went to twice-daily calls, with Fred joining in on the end of the conversation as my cheerleader, rooting me on to make the move happen as quickly as possible!

Everyone who cared about me thought that caring for both of my parents was a bad idea—a very bad idea. My head knew they were right, but my heart just couldn't turn its back on a man's dying wish. Especially if that wish was to be close to his only daughter. At least, that's what I told myself. I honestly thought he would find some grace in his last weeks on earth to be kind, considerate, and complimentary, three things I rarely saw from him while I was under his care. I reiterated that under no circumstances would he be able to live in my home with my mother. He said he understood, and at that, I moved him to a nursing home close to me, remarkably in just a few short weeks. He would be able to come to my home every day all day but return to the nursing home to sleep.

~

It was a warm day in April, at least by New England standards, as Tom, my mother, and I set out for the two-hour drive to get my father. I got out of the car to give him a quick greeting before returning to my mother, who remained in the front seat. Once again, the relocating of possessions from one place to another fell on Tom, and most of them were already in Dad's car, which Tom drove to our house. I followed in my car with my parents.

Dad had a feeding tube but was able to eat soft food, so I made him something to eat and let him relax a bit before taking him to the nursing home to check in. We settled into a routine of Tom bringing coffee and a paper to the nursing home on his way to work. Then my father would start calling me after eight o'clock each morning to ask when I was going to come and pick him up. If I didn't answer the phone because I was busy or wanted to sleep late, he called back every three minutes until I did. Sometimes he would call ten times before I finally answered. Within a few days, he was at my house from eight in the morning until eight at night. We took him to restaurants, family gatherings, parties, and holiday events, but it was never enough. He never wanted to go back to the nursing home; he wanted to stay with us.

Before long, my father was eating almost entirely by mouth and had no visible signs of dying anytime too soon. In fact, he was improving and thriving with the care he got from the nursing staff, Tom, and me. But his presence wasn't helping when it came to my mother's well-being. Dad's appearance had changed quite a bit. Sometimes Mom thought he was my father's brother, and other times, she called him "that man." I think he made her uncomfortable, although she was very kind to him. She would offer him something to eat, or a cup of coffee—neither of which she could fetch for him—but it was sweet of her just the same.

"I hope I never have to eat a ham sandwich in a tube," she said when he resorted to a can of liquid protein.

Caring for both my mother and father all day was getting very difficult. Neither of them could get themselves a glass of water, let alone a meal. But it was cleaning up after them that sent me over the edge. I was constantly picking tissues up off the floor and candy wrappers off tabletops. I didn't mind doing it for my mother; she'd cleaned up after people all her life. But my father was a different story. He was perfectly capable of picking up after himself, but he was lazy and selfish by nature. He never picked up after himself, or anyone—ever! Why should he change now?

One afternoon, I found a nut on the end table beside the couch where he was sitting. He'd sucked all the sugar off a Jordan Almond and left the nut on the table for me to clean up. I lost it! Discarded tissues, newspapers, coffee mugs and dishes to pick up, clothes to wash, puddles of liquid protein on the floor to clean, and that little nut was the thing that sent me into orbit!

"Dad, you mean to tell me you couldn't throw that nut away?" I interrogated.

"What nut?" he said.

"The one you left on the table while you were watching TV."

"I forgot."

"That's so disrespectful. You need to start helping out."

"I can do that."

I shook my head and walked away.

That was his mantra when I asked him to do something. "I can do that." It sounded humble and cooperative, but I was cautious. In the past, that comment had had a condescending connotation; besides, I was annoyed that I had to even ask at all.

Just as I feared, and thought I made perfectly clear wasn't going to happen, Dad continued his ploy to move in with me. It didn't matter how many times I told him I couldn't have him at my home full time, he wanted it, and he was going to do everything in his power to make it happen. His mind was remarkably good, and he had perfectly fine reasoning skills, unlike my mother, who had very little. He made it his mission to coax me into giving him permission to move in. He wanted to fall asleep on the couch in front of the fireplace just like he did when I was a kid. But I remembered how well he shared. I remembered how he took the room over. I remembered that when he was in the room, everyone else left.

And then I remembered that this was my home—not his.

One morning Mom got out of bed earlier than usual, so I reluctantly left her alone for ten minutes while I picked him up at the nursing home.

"Mom's home alone," I said, looking for some accolades. "I hate leaving her alone."

"Why? She's OK."

"I don't know how much longer I can care for her at home."

"Why don't you put her in the nursing home? She can take my bed, and I can come live with you."

I wondered quietly how after all the years of dealing with him, he could still surprise me with his narcissism.

"Would you have given up your life to take care of your mother or father?" I asked.

It was a rhetorical question, as he didn't take care of his wife or children, never mind his parents. "I don't know, I'd have to think about that," he replied.

"It's really hard, Dad."

"Don't you think Tom would give anything to have his parents around to take care of?"

"Actually, Tom is grateful that he never had to deal with how to care for his parents if they were no longer able to care for themselves. Yes, he would love to still have them in his life, but he also recognizes that caring for a parent full time is a lot of work and something neither one of his parents wanted for their children."

As he stared out the window contemplating our conversation, I wondered if I was doing the right thing by not bringing him into my home. But a minute later, I became irritated that once again he failed to be a little sympathetic or appreciative or simply acknowledge what I was sacrificing. It was all about what he wanted—it always was.

As Dad got stronger, I should have looked for more of an assisted-living situation for him. He really didn't belong in a nursing home. He showed no signs of dying soon, and his doctor was talking about removing the feeding tube. I had a lot on my plate, and before I could address the situation, he had a verbal altercation with his roommate and was asked to leave the nursing home.

"Peggy, your dad threatened to throw his roommate out the window," the social worker said.

"Great. That's just great," I replied.

"Well, I'm sure he didn't mean it, but we have to take these things seriously."

"Of course you do. I completely understand."

"He said he could live with you."

"He's wrong. He can't live with me."

"Oh?"

"I've made that perfectly clear to him. I can't take him in. I have my mother living here. She needs full-time care, and besides, he kind of freaks her out."

"OK, I'll start looking for a place for him to stay. Meanwhile, we've assigned someone to sit with him while he is alone in the room with Joe."

"I'm so sorry. I really am so sorry."

"It's not your fault. We'll figure it out."

The next morning, I had a conversation with my father. "Dad, you know, you're very fortunate that your mind is good and you are capable of doing what you desire," I said.

"Why can't I stay here?" he pleaded.

"You can't, Dad. Mom would love to go back to Florida. Obviously she can't, but you can," I added.

He just looked at me. Neither one of my parents had a penny or a plan.

"Dad, the social worker is looking for a place for you. But it will probably be about an hour away from here. What do you want to do?"

"I have lots of people in Florida who would love to take me in."

I heard loud and clear what he left out: "*So why won't you?*"

"You're lucky then. Why don't you go?"

"Fine, I'll just stay here a couple of weeks until I figure it out."

"Dad, you can't stay here. Your options are to let the social worker place you somewhere, or you make the choice yourself."

"Fine, I'll go to Florida then. I'll work it out."

"You'll lose your Medicaid."

"I don't care about that. The VA will take care of me. Especially with all the news about them in the spotlight."

And with that, he went to work on his plan.

He made a point to have his phone conversations with his buddies when I was near enough to hear him. They seemed a little flimsy to me, but I thought he understood his options. He took every opportunity to remind me about all the people who would do anything for him (unlike his cold-hearted daughter).

And then the plan was finalized. He was going to stay with his buddy Fred for a week or so until his buddy Pete was ready to travel south. Staying with Fred (who couldn't wait to get rid of him months earlier) should have been a red flag, but when it came to Dad's friends, I didn't expend much thought. His buddy Pete was going to drive him to South Carolina, coinciding with a trip to visit his brother. After that, Dad was going to put himself and his car on a train the rest of the way to Florida, where he was going to live with his buddy Jay. I reminded him that what little money he did have in savings went to the nursing home, but he assured me he would be fine. He always was.

My father was discharged on a beautiful Saturday morning in June. Tom went to pick him up.

"Thanks for everything," he said to the nurse on duty. "You gals were great, but at the rate this place charges, it should have come with a hooker every night."

Tom looked at the nurse and shook his head. "Geez, Paul," he said and escorted him out the door before he could insult anyone else. As he was driving away, the phone at our house rang.

"Peggy, it's Fred."

"Hi, Fred. What's up?" I wondered.

"Hey, I have no intention of taking your father in."

"Excuse me?" My heart sank all the way to my legs that wobbled under me.

"I can't take him in here. He's sick."

"Fred, he's been discharged. He doesn't have anyplace to go."

"Well, I can't have him here. What am I going to do if he gets really sick?"

"You couldn't have told me this earlier? You had no trouble calling me every day when you wanted him out of your house. Honestly, I don't understand you people."

"And Pete isn't going to drive him to South Carolina."

"Nice, Fred. Nice!"

I hung up the phone. I had no allegiance to him and after that conversation, not even enough respect to even say good-bye. I sat on my deck trying to process what had just happened when Tom came through the door with my father.

"Now what are you going to do?" I said to my father.

"What do you mean?" he said as if he didn't know.

"Fred called. He has no intentions of taking you in."

"He's a wimp."

"You knew."

"He'll take me in."

"No. He won't. Now you're homeless!"

"I'll just live with you for a little while until I figure it out."

"Dad, either you've been lying to me or they've been lying to you."

"What are you talking about? I've never lied to you."

"Well, let me tell you what I do know—the only one who hasn't been lying is me. I told you hundreds of times that you cannot live with me. So now you're homeless."

We sat in silence for a few minutes.

"You're going to have to find a hotel room until we can come up with a new plan," I said.

I knew that he manipulated the whole scene. I knew it! I also knew that if I let my guard down and gave him one night in my house, he would never leave. I was furious that he didn't believe me and even more upset that he brought me to a place of anger and nastiness. It simply wasn't fair.

There were times when I thought about taking him in. I told myself it would be temporary and the right thing to do. But minutes later, my thoughts turned physiological to a point where I actually felt sick. My body grew dark with fear, and I became paralyzed for a moment. Realizing that this darkness would overtake my life, I snapped myself back to reality. I stayed true to my original offer to help him as much as I could without taking him into my home.

"I'm going to drive to Fred's house," he announced.

"Dad, you can't do that," I replied.

"Why not?"

"How can you drive? You're sick."

"I can drive. I'm perfectly fine."

"Do whatever you want."

I said a prayer asking Saint Michael to go with him so he wouldn't hurt anyone.

"I'll lead you to the highway, Paul, and you can take it from there," Tom said.

"I don't think you should go all the way to Fred's house. I think you should get a room," I said.

"I'll be fine," my father replied.

Off they went.

I sat on the deck and prayed many prayers and then got in touch with my therapist, so she could talk me down a bit. I practiced breathing slower and prayed to calm my mind and heart. Ten minutes later, Tom came back with a somber look on his face and sat down next to me.

"What's wrong?" I asked.

"Peggy, I don't know how to tell you this, but your father didn't get on the highway."

"What do you mean?"

"He was right behind me. I got on the highway, and he went straight."

"I'm not surprised."

"He was sitting at the light with his arm out the window—sleeves rolled up—looking confident as all hell."

"He had no intention of getting on the highway," I said. I was numb. "He still intends to come back here."

"I'm sorry," Tom groaned.

"I'm not going to worry about it. That was his plan all along, but it's not going to happen. He can get a hotel room, or he can reach out to one of his many buddies. I'm not going to let him manipulate me."

The phone call I had anticipated came three hours later.

"Peg, I'm at the pub. I can't make it," my father said.

"Well, Dad, you need to find a place to stay, because you can't stay here."

"I'll just stay at your house for a couple of days until I figure things out."

"No, Dad, you will have to find a hotel room, because you can't stay here."

"Can't I just sleep on your couch?"

"No, you can't."

"I'll just sleep in my car in your driveway,"

"That's ridiculous! Get a hotel room and figure out what you're going to do."

"Fine," he groaned.

Later that day, I heard he made it to back to the town where Fred lived.

Thank God that chapter's over, I thought.

I was relieved to learn that he was safe and sound in the care of his buddies. I chose to believe him when he said he had lots of people who would be happy to take him in and chose to believe one of them would take pity on him and help him out.

I was wrong.

The next morning was a picture-perfect Sunday. Tom and I packed a cooler and some chairs and took Mom to watch two of our grandchildren play in an all-day lacrosse tournament. The beautiful field overlooked the ocean. The warm sun and cool breeze were both magical and calming, and the sound of little children running around was a delicious tonic. The saga with my father was over, and all was well with the world.

At the end of a wonderful day I felt like a ton of bricks was lifted off my shoulders. Tom went out to the garden to water the flowers while I prepared dinner. I came out on the deck to ask him a question, and while I was talking with him, I saw the life drain out of his face as he stood there motionless.

"What's the matter?" I asked.

He stood there speechless. I heard footsteps behind me and turned around to see Dad standing there.

"What the hell!" I screamed.

"I can't make it," he said calmly as he sat down.

"What do you mean? I thought you were with your buddies."

"I drove all the way to Brooklyn, slept in a Wal-Mart parking lot, had a bagel, and came back here."

I immediately felt sick and nervous and anxious and dark and dirty. "I don't want to do this, Dad."

How many times is he going to make me turn him away? Once is difficult enough, but hundreds is just awful! I lost it. I was a little child again, and Tom could see each and every emotion on my face.

"Why can't I just stay with you?"

"Because you can't!"

"I'll sleep on your couch."

The thought made me sick.

"Dad! You can't. You just can't!"

"Look," said Tom, "I have to go to DC on Tuesday. We'll get him a hotel room, book him a flight to Florida, and I'll take him to the airport on Tuesday. We'll transport his car down later."

"That's fine," my father said reluctantly.

"Do you actually have someone to stay with down there, or was that a lie too?" I asked.

"Yes, I have someone to stay with," he said.

In the middle of this debacle, our friends Jack and Diane came by as planned and watched as the scene unfolded. I was furious that I'd allowed my father to reduce me to feeling like a heartless, selfish shrew, but ironically for him, his success did me in. I had had enough and wanted him off my responsibility plate. The more I looked at him, the angrier I got, and he knew it. I tried very hard over and over again to be kind and considerate of his needs while recognizing my caregiving limits. But the whole time, it wasn't what he wanted to hear. The arrangement met his needs but not his wants, so he just kept pushing. Now, as he sat on the patio furniture, sick and exhausted, he knew the gig was over.

Tom got on the phone to book the hotel room, while I got on the computer to book his flight. Dad handed me his credit card, which was declined, so I used mine without his knowledge. Dad still didn't get it. He wanted to stay and visit with our friends.

"Can I have a beer?" he asked.

"No. Tom is going to take you to the hotel now," I said.

I was incensed by his attitude. Maybe the alcohol he had been drinking daily since his teens prevented his brain from developing properly. Perhaps it was a disorder. Or maybe he was just stubborn and selfish. Whatever the case may have been, I couldn't deal with him for one more minute. It was time for him to move on.

While I stayed home with our friends, Tom drove my father to a local hotel that he frequently used for traveling colleagues, so he knew the staff well. Tom introduced Dad to the manager and then brought him up to the restaurant/lounge and introduced him to the bartender.

"This is my father-in-law, Paul. Would you keep an eye on him?" he said to the bartender.

"Sure, no problem," he replied.

"If you have any questions or if he gives you any trouble, give me a call."

"We'll be fine, Tom."

One thousand dollars and two days later, my father was back in Florida. For a long time, I was happy for him, knowing that's where he wanted to be, until I realized months later that he didn't want to be in Florida at all—he wanted to be with family. He just didn't want it enough to compromise.

FIFTEEN

A clear conscience is a soft pillow.

—My grandma

A YEAR HAD passed since I cried tears of joy while reading the text from Matthew.

"She said yes!"

Now with their wedding day just ten weeks away, my beautiful, soon-to-be daughter-in-law Laura and I sat down together to go over plans. Like a ton of bricks falling on my head, I realized just how little of myself I had given to her throughout the year. "I'm so sorry that I haven't been there for you," I said.

"That's OK, but please tell me you will follow your plan and not bring Nonni back here if she goes to the nursing home again," Laura said.

"I promise. Really, I promise."

One of Laura's most endearing qualities was that when others thought it, Laura said it!

"I know. It's time," I added.

I missed every family get-together that year.

For over a year, my family and I talked about placing my mother in long-term care, but I wasn't ready. I knew once Mom left my home, I would be forced to deal with the truth. My mother was dying. It *was* getting close to the point where I could no longer care for her in my home, but I couldn't even *think* of taking her to a nursing home, never mind actually put her in a car and drive her there. She had an awful reaction with the two visits to the neurologist, thinking she was going to a long-term care facility, and I still felt the sting. The memory of denying my father a warm bed in my home added to the guilt I struggled with; there was no way I could live with denying my mother one. I just wouldn't. I thought of all sorts of ways to get her into long-term care, and every one of them made me uncomfortable.

"Just put her in the car and take her," my friend Bobby said.

"Get a 'chair car' and tell her she's going for rehab," a friend suggested during a conversation at a gathering.

"What's a 'chair car?'" I asked.

"It's a car service that you can hire to transport people who need a wheelchair."

"Oh, so it's an ambulance?"

"Well, yes, but for rent."

"You have to just do it!" Bobby said in a firm tone.

~

Months later when my brother Tim was visiting, I made pizza and salad for dinner while Mom worked overtime to impress upon Tim that she was perfectly fine and disease-free.

"Mom, you shouldn't eat that pizza. I made the cheeseless pizza for you," I ordered.

"That's just bread and sauce," she complained.

"I know, but you shouldn't have the cheese."

"There's no flavor without the cheese!"

"You've been pulling the cheese off pizza for years."

"Well, I'm in charge of what I eat."

"Yes, you are, but—" I stopped with a sigh and went into another room.

Just as I feared, I spent the next four days trying to get her to poop.

"Are you keeping track of these beans?" she asked. It drove me crazy when she refused to accept help and then yelled at me when the damage was done.

"You have to drink the prune juice I make for you," I said.

"I do."

"No. You save it for later, and I throw it away."

"Only when there are bugs in it."

"I can't force you to drink the prune juice. I can't force you to eat the cheeseless pizza. I can't force you to take the cranberry pills. But if you don't take my advice, this is what happens. You get constipated, and then you get a UTI."

She just stared at me.

I felt a whole lot of panic, splashed with a little bit of relief, and a whole lot more panic. My heart was so heavy that I couldn't fully breathe. The space between my shoulders carried a heavy weight and was constantly in pain. I knew within days Mom would be in the hospital and out of my home forever. I felt like a pinball machine with a little silver ball inside me hitting the full range of emotions, running through my body and exploding them one at a time. *How could I let this happen to her?* I felt sad, angry, hurt, scared, fearful, panicked, liberated, and anxious.

For days, I worked on making mental preparations as I watched her demise play out in front of me. I had to keep my promise, and it scared me to death. Two weeks later, Mom needed an unscheduled shower, which I reluctantly gave her because she was unsteady. After we finished, I took my hand off her just long enough to reach for the towel when she fell. She didn't fall hard, but she started complaining later that afternoon, so with a broken heart, I took her to the ER.

I'm not ready.

I wondered if I would ever be ready. I did everything I could to make it work, but I couldn't manage to care for everyone. Someone's needs went ignored—my children, grandchildren, friends, parties, Tom's, mine.

I knew all about the sacrifices my loved ones were making, but I wasn't ready.

Mom sat slumped over in a wheelchair in the ER lobby with a neck brace and slightly soiled clothes for five hours before getting through the massive doors. When she started sundowning at four thirty I thought about bringing her home. I thought about it again when her bedtime hour approached at six thirty, but every time I tried to straighten out her twisted body, she moaned. So as awful as it was, we sat there, each in our own individual hell, and we waited. When she finally got a bed in the ER, they ran some tests, and shortly after 11:00 p.m., they told me we could go home.

"You want me to take her home now?" I said to the nurse.

"I know. It doesn't seem right, but they can't find a reason to admit her," she replied.

"My husband is away. I have to get her in the car by myself, get her in the house by myself, clean her up by myself, and get her into bed by myself?"

"I'm sorry."

She left the room, and I called my sister-in-law Lynne.

"They want me to take her home now," I said through tears.

"Oh no, honey, you can't do that," Lynne replied.

"I know I can't, but what can I do? They said they don't have a reason to admit her."

"Ask to speak to a social worker. Tell the social worker that you're not comfortable taking her home."

"Really? I can do that?"

"Yes. Just tell them that you can't give her proper care tonight, and you want her to stay."

"Then what?"

"One day at a time. See how she is tomorrow. If she's better, that's great. But at least you won't be taking her home at midnight."

"Thank you, my angel. Thank you. Thank you."

"No problem, Peg. Keep me posted."

The conversation with the social worker lasted not more than three minutes. She didn't need much persuasion. She knew that it was not in anyone's best interest to transport a sick, elderly woman in the middle of the night without any help. Mom stayed, and I went home.

The next morning, I learned that Mom had been dreadful to the ER nurses.

"I was sure she had a UTI. In fact," I said, "I still am."

"I agree. We sent off a sample to be tested," said the nurse.

I wondered if they performed the test the night before as I had requested. I turned around to walk to Mom's room and literally ran into the social worker on duty.

"Hello, I'm Joan, the social worker," she said.

"Hi, how—" I said before she gently interrupted me.

"Would you give me a few minutes? I need to review some things before we talk."

"Of course. I'll just go and sit with her for a while."

"Great. I'll come find you."

Mom was sitting in an upright position with one foot dangling over the side of the bed, and she was downright nasty. She seemed to be lost in a fury of complete and utter pandemonium. It was as if she swallowed a bottle of jumping beans and they were pinging every cell in her body over and over, and she couldn't find any relief.

"Peggy, get me the hell out of here. Now! I'm not staying here," she said desperately.

"OK, Mom, calm down," I said.

"I am *not* staying here."

"I'll be right back."

I quickly walked out of the room and kept walking until I saw Joan the social worker again.

"Are you looking for me?" I asked.

"Yes. There is no need for us to meet. Your mom has a UTI, so they're going to admit her. I wanted to get the results before we talked," she said.

I closed my eyes and said a prayer of thanks. I wasn't looking forward to taking her home in that condition, long term or short.

"I figured as much," said another nurse listening from a distance.

The social worker left, and I walked back to Mom's room with the nurse, but before I got there, I stopped in my tracks.

"I am so sorry, but I can't go back in there. She's really mad," I said.

"No. It's probably best if you just go."

"I feel awful, but sometimes I just make matters worse."

"I saw that, and I agree."

"I'm sorry. When she has a UTI she yells, bites, kicks, screams, and swears something awful. I even saw her spit once."

"Don't worry. We can handle her."

"But she really is very sweet when she's well."

"Get me the hell outta here!" Mom yelled from her bed.

"We've seen this before. Go home," said the nurse.

I left for the day.

Mom spent two more nights on the seventh floor, giving her the required three nights in order to go to rehab. In those two days, her behavior was anything but typical. She was either sad and reflective or angry and nasty. I spent as little time as possible visiting her. I think a part of her knew she would not be returning home.

"I don't think I look old enough to go into a nursing home," Mom explained to me softly, almost childlike.

"You don't. You're absolutely beautiful. You look better than I do," I replied.

"But—my age isn't ready to go to a nursing home." She was struggling to find the right words.

"I know, Mom, but it's not about age. You can't take care of yourself. You have to be able to take care of yourself."

"Well, if I had money, I could."

I lied. "Mom, you only have to go for a little while so you can get stronger. Then you can come back home."

We sat together in a quiet, tender, loving place until it happened. Like someone flicked a switch in her brain, Lewy appeared.

"I don't think we should wait for lunch. Let's go home now," she decided.

"No, Mom, you have to stay for a couple of days."

"I think we should go."

"They have to treat you, and then we can go."

She stared at me with her pensive blue eyes.

"I'm going to go now, but I will be right back," I lied again.

"OK, we'll have lunch at the end of the week," she said.

~

My father lived more than a year longer than doctors predicted. He was with his buddy for three months before wearing out his welcome, and after that, he was admitted to the hospital for failure to thrive. He spent the remainder of his life going between a VA hospital and a VA nursing home, where great people took very good care of him. The "plenty of friends who would love to take him in" suddenly disappeared, and his family was too far away to visit. During one phone conversation, he told me he was lonely.

"You're what?" I asked.

"Never mind," he said. It was too late. We would both have to find a way to make peace with our decisions. The decisions didn't seem to faze him; he still called me "baby" when we spoke on the phone. But the decisions I made continued to tug at my heartstrings, adding to my feelings of parental betrayal.

During my Florida stay in February 2015, my objective was to treat myself to a much-needed retreat. I wanted a full twenty-one days to practice, so I added two days on each end of my three-week stay for settling in, cleaning up, and travel. I brought books, prayer cards, meditation tapes, and held a vigil to my parents with white candles in front of a picture of Mother Mary. I ate fresh food, drank lots of water, slept, prayed, walked, swam, read, meditated all alone, and listened to the universe every day. On my morning walk, I prayed quietly, stopping to sit in front of the little pond at the marina store to chat with the turtles, and on my afternoon walk, I took my music and sang out loud.

Halfway through my retreat I learned that Dad was feeling very sick and told his doctor he didn't want to continue with any further treatments. Days later, he went to the hospice unit. There they would keep him comfortable until he passed. For many days I called a number of times each day to see how he was doing while I waited. Finally, feeling like a penned-up animal, I had to get out of my home, so I called the hospice person on duty and told them I was going out, and if they needed me, they should call my cell phone.

"He's awake," the hospice nurse said. "Would you like to speak with him?"

"Sure," I said with a heavy heart.

He couldn't speak, and his breathing was really labored, so I did all the talking. "Daddy, you did the best you could. You fought a good fight, but it's time to go. Close your eyes and look for the white light. When you see the white light, go to it. It's God, and He's there for you. He'll take you in His arms and wrap you up in His love."

He couldn't respond with words; he acknowledged me with moans.

"I love you, Daddy. It's all OK. It's time to go."

I repeated those words over and over, and I meant every word. The one-way conversation lasted only about four minutes, but seemed like forever as I waited for the nurse to take the phone away from his ear. Finally, I had to end the painful conversation so I let the last words be, "Go to the white light, Daddy. God loves you. God will take care of you. I promise."

Dad was also in Florida, but I couldn't bring myself to make the four-hour drive alone to be with him and sit vigil while I waited for him to pass. With no one to accompany me on the drive and no one to stay with while there, I couldn't go through it alone. It was just too much for me to handle, although I did feel closer to him just by being in the same state. At the end of the somber phone conversation, I picked up my bag, towel, and headphones, and left to sit by the pool for a couple of hours. I made the five-minute walk across the street to the community pool and took another five minutes to settle into my chosen spot and apply sunscreen. I was just about to get lost in my headphones with Deepak and Oprah when my cell phone rang. It was Dad's hospice nurse.

"Hello?"

"I'm so sorry, Peggy, but your father just passed," she said.

"Oh! OK, thank you for calling. And thank you for everything you did for my father," I said.

"He must've needed to hear what you had to say, because he passed minutes after you spoke with him."

My father, Paul Daniel, died on my Daniel Paul's birthday. With no rush to make funeral plans, I decided to stay in Florida for the remainder of my trip. My brother, my husband, and my son were all out to sea, so I had to wait for three ships to get to port.

~

As I sat in the back seat of the Town Car, looking out the window, I watched the familiar landmarks passing by, distorted through my tears and showing me the way to the airport that would take me home. With Dad gone and Mom in long-term care, my life changed dramatically. They were no longer my responsibility. I was having a difficult time sorting out all the emotions jumping back and forth from my head to my heart, when suddenly I broke out in a big smile. I noticed that I was consistently rocking, falling forward, and crashing backward into the seat. My driver was stepping on the gas forcefully and releasing it abruptly for the first ten minutes of the trip before he found a steady pace on the highway.

I knew it was a message from Dad. He did the same thing and achieved the same response when I was a child—a smile from heaven.

Coming home to an empty house for a few days before Tom returned home from sea gave me time to reflect on the past five years of my journey with Mom. Now done with the caregiving role, I had the opportunity to breathe and admire my accomplishments. Oh yes, I certainly had failures, but I like to think of them as lessons—like the lessons Mom gave me while raising my children; lessons that I was grateful to have, privileged to have. Lessons that provided me with one more day with Mom.

We all have to live our own lives and walk our own journeys. I personally needed a good amount of help with the *Lewy, Mom, and Me* journey, and fortunately, I had the strength to ask. I received many great gifts and answers in the form of the perfect people to help. My mother made her very difficult journey filled with her own set of people, gifts, and lessons. All the people who were touched by my mother were intertwined into the fabric of her life, as she was into ours, and we each have our own unique blanket. I will treasure mine forever.

Epilogue

TWO YEARS AGO, when Mom entered into long-term care in the nursing home, I had a heart-to-heart chat with the nurse who processed her admission papers. I was a mess—asking questions that had no answers and searching for a timeline that didn't exist.

"Nora, I'm completely lost," I said.

"Don't worry about it today. You'll figure it out," she replied.

It only took a few weeks of observing the wonderful staff tending to Mom before they earned my complete trust. I saw them interact with her every day when I brought her lunch and sometimes twice a day when I brought dinner too. I popped in to pick up her laundry and a few times a week to bring her a sweet treat. In those early days, it wasn't uncommon for me to make three or four trips a day to be with Mom. Concerned friends suggested I reduce the level of caregiving I was providing, telling me it was time to regain my own life. But I honestly didn't think she would live more than a few months, and I wanted to be with her as much as possible. When those few months came and went, I had another heart-to-heart with Nora.

"What's going on with Mom?" I asked her. "How long do you think she'll live?"

"I can't tell you that, Peggy. What I can tell you is what happens with all the other caregivers who have loved ones here."

"What?"

"They start off visiting daily. As time goes on, their visits become less frequent. Eventually your mom won't recognize you, and not long after that, she will pass."

A year later, Mom had her first bout of clostridium difficile colitis (C. diff.), a gastrointestinal infection. It's a painful infection and known to take many lives in the elderly community. Mom fought off three. I wasn't allowed to take her laundry home when she was first diagnosed. Six weeks later, Nora took me aside.

"Peggy, we tested your Mom yesterday. She's great, but we'll keep her on probiotics," she said.

"That's good," I whispered.

"Why don't you let us continue to do her laundry? Take it off your plate."

I gave up doing the laundry and began visiting only once a day. Mom eventually stopped asking me to take her home. She began referring to the nursing home as a hotel. She was able to have lengthy conversations with intelligence, mixed with hallucinated gibberish.

Mom also weathered a number of UTIs. And twenty months after she was admitted, she fell and had to have a hip replacement. She returned and had therapy for a few months, but she never fully recovered, spending more and more time in a wheelchair. Today she goes from her bed to her wheelchair to her bed. She's on hospice, sometimes goes days without fully waking, then has days where she is very alert and hungry. She doesn't recognize faces, but she does respond to familiar names. I can get her to smile every time I see her, even while I'm holding back tears. I've learned to accept as much as I can process with each new day, and to cherish the rare moments when the old Francesca comes out to visit. When I met with the hospice team, they asked about her likes and dislikes. I told them she does *not* like anything but clear nail polish on her fingers. I made it quite clear, but somehow the message got lost. Days later, when I walked into the room to see that her frail little hands had bright red-orange nail polish on their fingernails, I was shocked.

"What's this, Mom? You hate color on your nails," I said.

"She insisted," she whispered. Her voice was so faint I often had to put my ear to her lips to hear her words.

"Why didn't you just say no?"

"I tried, but I didn't want to take a vote."

"Do you like it?"

"No."

As I returned to the nursing home to visit her the next day, I realized I forgot to bring nail polish remover. Hoping she wouldn't notice until I came back with it the next day, I sat down next to her and gave her some chocolates.

"Junior prom," she said as she lifted her hands like a bunny rabbit.

"I know, right?" I laughed. *That's my girl,* I thought.

I will miss my mother terribly. I already do. But I will carry her love in my heart forever.

> "At the moment of death, we will not be judged accord-
> ing to the number of good deeds we have done or by
> the diplomas we have received in our lifetime. We will be
> judged according to the love we have put into our work."
>
> —MOTHER TERESA

Made in the USA
Columbia, SC
02 August 2017